be your own career consultant

WORK OUT
WANT TO BE

WHERE YOU
AND GET THERE

be your own career consultant

how to unlock your career potential
and help yourself to your future

Gary Pyke
Stuart Neath

www.yourmomentum.com
the stuff that drives you

What is momentum?

Momentum is a completely new publishing philosophy, in print and online, dedicated to giving you more of the information, inspiration and drive to enhance who you are, what you do, and how you do it.

Fusing the changing forces of work, life and technology, momentum will give you the right stuff for a brighter future and set you on the way to being all you can be.

Who needs momentum?

Momentum is for people who want to make things happen in their careers and their lives, who want to work at something they enjoy and that's worthy of their talents and their time.

Momentum people have values and principles, and question who they are, what they do, and who for. Wherever they work, they want to feel proud of what they do. And they are hungry for information, stimulation, ideas and answers …

Momentum online

Visit *www.yourmomentum.com* to be part of the talent community. Here you'll find a full listing of current and future books, an archive of articles by momentum authors, sample chapters and self-assessment tools. While you're there, post your work/life questions to our momentum coaches and sign up to receive free newsletters with even more stuff to drive you.

If you need more drive for your life, try one of these other momentum titles:

soultrader
personal career strategies for life
Carmel McConnell

mental space
how to find clarity in a complex life
Tina Konstant and Morris Taylor

reinvent yourself
tactics for work, life and happiness - yours
J. Jonathan Gabay

managing brand me
how to build your personal brand
Thomas Gad and
Anette Rosencreutz

coach yourself
make real change in your life
Anthony M. Grant and Jane Greene

change activist
make big things happen fast
Carmel McConnell

lead yourself
be where others will follow
Mick Cope

happy mondays
putting the pleasure back into work
Richard Reeves

innervation
redesign yourself for a smarter future
Guy Browning

the big difference
life works when you choose it
Nicola Phillips

hey you!
pitch to win in an ideas economy
Will Murray

snap, crackle or stop
change your career and create your own destiny
Barbara Quinn

float you
how to capitalize on your talent
Carmel McConnell and Mick Cope

from here to e
equip yourself for a career in the wired economy
Lisa Khoo

grow your personal capital
what you know, who you know and how you use it
Hilarie Owen

PEARSON EDUCATION LIMITED

Head Office
Edinburgh Gate
Harlow CM20 2JE
Tel: +44 (0)1279 623623
Fax: +44 (0)1279 431059

London Office:
128 Long Acre, London WC2E 9AN
Tel: +44 (0)20 7447 2000
Fax: +44 (0)20 7240 5771
Website: www.business-minds.com

First published in Great Britain in 2002

The right of Gary Pyke and Stuart Neath to be identified as Authors of this Work has been asserted by them in accordance with the Copyright, Designs and Patents Act 1988.

ISBN 1843 04020 4

British Library Cataloguing in Publication Data
A CIP catalogue record for this book can be obtained from the British Library.

10 9 8 7 6 5 4 3 2 1

Typeset by Northern Phototypesetting Co. Ltd, Bolton
Printed and bound in Great Britain by Henry Ling Ltd, Dorchester

Production design by Claire Brodmann Book Designs, Lichfield, Staffs.

The Publishers' policy is to use paper manufactured from sustainable forests.

Thank you…

from Gary

My thanks first to Stuart for making this journey with me, for believing in the idea we had and sticking with it as we made it happen.

To Mick Cope for being 'Mick', nuff said – one Great Thing! To Rachael Stock and Amanda Thompson for all their help and support – another Great Thing!

Also to anybody who I have bounced ideas off for the past two years, including the Northern Development Group (Mark, Hayley, Caroline, Michelle, Mike, Kevin), Derek and Ffyona.

Finally to Jo, Tegan and Aimee for being there.

from Stuart

Thank you to Mick Cope for challenging me every day. Thank you to Rachael and Amanda for listening to our ideas and enthusing about enough of them to encourage us to make this journey.

Thank you to Ffyona and Fiona ('Vange' and 'Hodge') for letting me throw ideas at them and for not laughing at me when I was colouring outside the lines. Thank you to everyone who has attended a workshop I have been involved in, for your input and feedback and for making me believe that we were doing something right.

Thank you to Slitty for the opening line.

Finally, thank you Gary, for helping me to explore ideas and pushing me to achieve a There & Then that I thought was beyond me. You are always a positive influence.

contents

preface

How can this book help?

First, a little background. In 1997 the authors were brought together as part of a small team to help deliver a course aimed at teaching people how to take ownership and responsibility for their own careers within a given organization. Happy and excited to do so, we joined in, got briefed and were asked to go away and run two courses back-to-back. By the end of the second course we knew that we had a major job on our hands.

The course did not hang together and had little or no common thread. There was some unfortunate use of negative terminology and words, and some of the tools and techniques needed upgrading, throwing away or rewriting. We then set about rewriting and redesigning large sections of the course, including the basic premise on which it was based. Once done, the course has continued to run until the present day, with the feedback from delegates being almost unanimously excellent.

This book is a reflection of that course and contains much of what we have incorporated into it. Our experience over the last five years is that *it works*. We hope that it will work for you.

introduction

'Once upon a time …'

There is a strange irony in our writing this book. You see, our experience tells us that many of us (ourselves included) are extremely sceptical about so-called 'self-help' books. We know that we are not alone in being extremely disappointed by the vast majority of such books that we have read. They usually fail to deliver even part of what they promise on the cover or in the advertising, reducing themselves to fiction.

It's therefore ironic that, sceptical as we are, we have decided that we can do it better, that the work we have been involved in for the last few years has led us to believe that we have something here which will genuinely add value for the reader. It's ironic that we should choose to write a book for one of the most critical audiences an author can approach.

If you are a sceptic like us, thank you for buying this book and please go on and read it. See if we are right, or whether the most appropriate line in the book is the opening one: 'Once upon a time …'

01

chapter one
careers happen

Signs of the times

Dickens wrote: 'It was the best of times, it was the worst of times ...'
But for you and for us, what times are we in now?

If Dickens was writing this today, we would probably be in the
fastest of times. Why? Because we live in a time in which speed is a
major deciding factor. There can be no doubt that these are fast-
moving, dynamic times and we have to be just as fast-moving and
dynamic to keep up!

Why do we say that? We see evidence everywhere around us that the
world is speeding up, getting faster and faster as it has done every
year for the last 60 years. And it is cumulative – each change seems
to speed the next until we have become a blur of activity. We see this
reflected in myriad statements in today's media:

◆ Computing power doubles every 18 months.

◆ You are only as good as the last result you produced.

◆ The job is becoming finite, and some say it's already dead.

◆ The time from conception to market is becoming months (even
  days), not years.

◆ We talk of first-mover advantage.

◆ There is a large increase in the number of 'virtual' businesses,
  with more and more employees working from home or from
  independent locations, away from an expansive and expensive
  central office.

◆ Companies are *morphed* (small moves linked to gain short-term growth opportunity) and *patched* (restitched to match market opportunities) or *time-paced* (constant rhythms of change to increase speed and momentum).

'The nineties will be a decade in a hurry, a nanosecond culture. There'll be only two kinds of managers: the quick and the dead.'

David Vice

If that was the nineties, what's happening now? The companies we work in are changing ever faster and we are in danger of being left behind. Why? Because if we're not careful, the next change the company makes may be one that does not need our skills or knowledge.

The question we face is: 'What can we do about it?' What can we do to make sure that we maintain or improve our position, now and in the future? In this ever-changing landscape, how can we ensure that we are equipped to change pace at the same rate?

Let's stop for a moment and think about the pace at which businesses have to adapt in the twenty-second century.

Sony

In his autobiography *Made in Japan*, Akio Morito, a founder of Sony, tells of how competitors have had to adapt to Sony's success:

'In the beginning, when our track record for success was not established, our competitors would take a very cautious wait-and-see attitude while we marketed and developed a new product. In the early days, we would often have the market to ourselves for a year or more before the other companies would be convinced that the product would be a success. And we made a lot of money, having the market all to ourselves. But as we became more successful and our track record became clearer, the others waited a shorter and shorter time before jumping in. Now we barely get a three-month head start on some products before the others enter the market to compete with us with their own version of the product we innovated. (We were fortunate to get a whole year's lead on the portable compact disc player, Discman, and almost six months with the Walkman.) It is flattering in a way, but it is expensive. We have to keep a premium on innovation.'

He goes on to say:

'Our plan is to lead the public with new products rather than ask them what kind of products they want. The public does not know what is possible, but we do. So instead of doing a lot of market research, we refine our thinking on a product and its use and try to create a market for it by educating and communicating with the public.'

Morito's book was published in 1986. How much faster does business move now? If Sony introduce a new product, how long do you think it is now before their competitors have a version of the same product on the market? A month? Two weeks? A week?

Large businesses have whole research departments dedicated to monitoring what their competitors are doing, what's new in the market, where the gaps are or where they can create new ones. Business has to move extremely quickly now, not only to get new products out ahead of competitors but also in reacting to competitor advances. Failure to react quickly enough can result in loss of market share with resultant negative impact on the business. In some cases this reduction in market share can have catastrophic results for everyone involved in the business from shareholders and senior management to workforce. *We only have to look at the problems Marks & Spencer have had in recent years to see how damaging loss of market share can be.*

Question! Living and working in this fast-paced world we have had to ask ourselves: 'What can we do to survive in this storm in which we live?' The answer begins with learning to manage ourselves and to improve our understanding of the environment in which we work. It is only by raising our awareness, by taking ownership and responsibility for our lives, and by recognizing the constant change going on around us that we can succeed in a fast-paced world. We have to be paying ever closer attention to the ebbs and flows of what is going on around us to understand how we can prosper within it.

At the time of writing, the company we work for has undergone a full company reorganization and company name change. Each operating unit has been assessed according to how it fits with the company vision and many units are now being outsourced. Where has that left us? Pretty much in the same position as many of you. That is, having to rely on matching our skills to the business and to its new aims, as well as looking to where the next change will happen.

What is unusual about this is that the company we work for has been around for a long, long time. It's not just in the e-world that change is occurring ever faster, but also in those industries in which change was seen as anathema. As globalization pushes each business to examine itself, change becomes the one and only constant. As every business examines how it can make more return on its investments, the one thing that often is lost in the process is the people – they become a commodity to be traded or removed from the equation.

Life just isn't stable any more, is it?

It's not standing still, and it certainly isn't waiting to hand you a fantastic job, in a fantastic place, giving you a fantastic life.

'And you may ask yourself – how did I get here?'

'Once in a Lifetime', David Byrne, Talking Heads

It's a question that strikes people particularly if they step back and see business turmoil happening around them – then there is a sudden realization that they are not where they expected to be. Particularly disturbing is the fact that the vast majority of change interventions (business reorganizations and so on) actually fail. There may be differences in the short term, but invariably these changes are not 'sticky'; before you know it everyone reverts to the old systems and structures.

It is estimated that 80% of change interventions within business fail, except in the IT industry, where the failure rate goes up to 90%, and the diet industry, where it reaches 99%. (If you want to find ways of making change more sustainable we recommend Mick Cope's *The Seven Cs of Consulting*.)

So many changes fail because businesses seldom make allowances for the intangible aspects of change: What is happening with the people involved? Are they happy with the changes? Do they buy into them? And most importantly, will they be happy to work with them once they have been implemented?

All changes impact on people, and if the organizations that impose those changes are not considering their people (i.e. us), then we have to ensure that we are looking after ourselves.

So, given a world in turmoil, and the fact that most of us are not where we want to be, what can we do about it?

There are books and there are more books that talk about personal change, about life change and about the promise of a brand new you. There are others that tell you about careers, what to do about them and how to get one. And finally there are others that tell you about the world that we are in today.

You can attempt to read them all and put into practice the lessons and ideas they propose. We've done that – and, to put it politely, what a fantastic bookend some of them make. The trouble with books (possibly even this one) is that they are often difficult to apply in real life. Why? Because most situations you get into are not the same as those stated in the books.

Why plan your career?

Because in the current environment if you are not doing it, who is? It's certainly not your Personnel Department. They have gone the way of many other departments: measured on the number of transactions they perform, the price they can get for a training course (the cheaper the better) and what they cost as an overhead compared to the investment in them (again, the cheaper the better).

And what of your Line Manager? Again, the answer is that they are probably dealing with a number of conflicting goals, many similar to the Personnel Department. These could be:

◆ What benefit are they adding to the company bottom line?

◆ Has the department hit its targets this month?

◆ Is everyone in the team hitting utilization targets?

◆ Will I get my bonus this year?

◆ Who will take the blame if I have not hit any of the previous three goals?

◆ What am I going to do about my own career, my own future, and how can I protect myself or get that next promotion or pay rise?

If you are lucky, you may find that you have a Line Manager who, once they have dealt with everything else, can find time to give some consideration to *your* future and where your career is heading.

So who is managing your career in the corporate world today? *You are!* And if you're not, then nobody else is. Nobody else can understand where you are now and how you feel about that. They can't understand your dreams and needs or what balance you need to strike between your work and your lifestyle. If you have bought this book, then hopefully you are already aware that if you aren't doing it then nobody else will.

be your own career consultant

momentum

Reality check

Who knows you better than you? Does your Line Manager really understand all your needs and aspirations? Does your Line Manager give you the time and support that you need to be able to plan your career and your development needs effectively and robustly?

If the answer is 'yes', then you are both very rare and extremely lucky. For the majority of us, the answer is 'no'. In these fast-moving times our Line Managers are so busy dealing with other stuff and also trying to look after their own interests that they can't give us all the time that we need.

Career planning and development comes at a price, and the cost is measured in time. Let's get it straight now, this stuff takes time to do it properly, and if we are not being given that time by our employers, then we *have* to do it for ourselves!

In most cases companies are handing back to employees the issue of career planning and everything that goes with it. The reason for this is that the contract between companies and their employees has changed. In the world today compared to the world of yesterday, a company can no longer guarantee the proverbial 'job for life'. In the fast pace of today, in order to stay nimble, companies need to be flexible to changing markets, fickle customers and globalization.

'Companies can no longer offer their employees cradle to grave job security. They are no longer able to take a school leaver or graduate and offer to guide them right through their career until retirement.

This fundamental truth has been dawning on many companies for several years, although they have taken some time to admit it, either to themselves or to the outside world, but the majority of individuals have still not grasped what this is going to mean to them.'

Bridget Wright, *Career Shift*

Here's another.

'There is no longer a set pathway in a career to getting to where you want to be, because you can no longer rely on an employer's loyalty or consistency. There is no longer a permanent job in the old sense of the word.'

Sue Read

Amanda's story

Amanda had been working in a family business for many years. She liked the work and the people, but she felt frustrated in her role and wanted to try a new challenge. Being a very sociable and outgoing person, Amanda decided that she should work in Sales, an area that many of her friends and associates agreed that she'd be good in.

Having spent some time writing up her CV and preparing for interviews, Amanda started applying for jobs. She was delighted to find herself being invited for a number of interviews, and even receiving a couple of job offers. But what Amanda found unusual was that the companies offering her work were also giving her sole responsibility for her development within the role. The way it worked was like this:

◆ At the start of the financial year Amanda would be given her own development budget as part of her package.

◆ She had to monitor the strategic direction and needs of the business. Based on what she thought would benefit the business and her own aspirations within it, she would then have to decide what development she needed, organize it and manage it whilst carrying out her job.

◆ At the end of the year Amanda would have to demonstrate that she had used the development budget effectively, reflecting the needs of the industry, the business, the customers and her own role and aspirations. Failure to do so would result in the budget being taken out of any bonuses due for the year or a reduction in the budget made available for the following year.

Amanda was not used to, or prepared for, this responsibility and found it too daunting. She still works for her family's business and is still frustrated.

This approach to development is not unusual nowadays. Check the Appointment pages in any broadsheet newspaper and you will see it referred to as part of the package that more and more businesses are offering.

Why be your own Career Consultant?

Because you have to be. You have no choice. You can choose to let life drift on as it has done and find yourself falling behind, or you can choose to do something about it. What you cannot afford to do is to give away decisions that impact upon your life and your future. The only person who can own their life is you!

Given the environment we live in, it will only be the conscious control of, or awareness of, your environment that will result in career success. You can't stop world events happening or your employer's business from changing, but by looking for signs and realizing that change is coming you can chart the path you want, either away from change or towards it. You need to decide on your course and know where you want to go.

'In field events you stand on the run-up on your own, and you are very much on your own.'

Jonathan Edwards – Triple Jumper, Olympic Gold Medal winner and World Champion

Given the change of contract between the employer and the worker, it's time to stand on your own. Management of your career is a field event. The contract has changed because it is having to take into account all the things that are happening in these fast times. The contract has become a 'deal' between you and the organization, demanding flexibility, dynamism and innovation. More than that, it demands more from you in terms of your commitment to the business.

Stuart's story

Stuart joined an extremely large company to work for them as an Operational Project Manager. On joining, he signed a contract agreeing to work 37.5 hours per week (i.e. a fairly standard 9–5.30 contract). He was told that his time would be split between chargeable hours (working for customers, bringing money into the business) and non-chargeable (time spent on administrative stuff – timesheets, management meetings, team meetings, holidays, training, etc.). No problems here until Stuart was told that his utilization target (the amount of time that he *must* spend on chargeable work) was 75% and that this was a bonus target for him. If he did not spend 75% of his time bringing in chargeable work, he would lose a portion of his bonus. But Stuart was also told that his non-chargeable time should be approximately 30%.

75% + 30% = 105%. Stuart checked, even to the point of questioning the Finance Director personally, and whichever way it was described to him, Stuart found that he was actually being told to work 56 weeks a year at 37.5 hours per week. This was not what was in his contract and when he challenged it the answer he was given was:

> 'We know, but as a manager it is just expected of you to work the extra hours as a demonstration of your loyalty and commitment to the business. The contract is a base document, but it forms just part of *the deal* that we have with you. We expect you to work the extra hours, but in return we give you a contract that pays you a good salary, gives you paid holidays and sick leave, training if you need it, equipment for your job and any technical support you need, and so on. Much of this is not included in the contract either, but we accept it as our responsibility, along with giving you a degree of job security.'

There is more to a contract now than ever before.

What do you need?

Most books gloss over the fact that when you make a decision there are both positive and negative consequences. Most of us like to take the positive and ignore the possible downsides, downsides that we need to be aware of in order to get what we want. We're not saying that it's wrong to focus on the positive, but you also need to be aware of the downside, the price you may have to pay, the *So What?* of the decision that you have made. If you don't, you won't be making robust decisions based on all the facts. We'll look at the 'So What?' later.

First, let us give you something to consider before we go on. We need you to consider the three Whats. That is:

1 What are your values?

2 What makes you feel valued?

3 What do you consider your value to be?

Start thinking about what it is that you want to satisfy.

Or, from another angle – people do things for different reasons. Why?

◆ **Values:** Because people have different values. Different things are important to them. People want different things.

◆ **Valued:** People feel valued in different ways because of their own, personal values: some need a large salary, others a big car and some a life without stress.

◆ **Value:** People need to know their value: to their employers, families and friends. If they don't, how are they going to be motivated or inspired to add any value to that 'relationship'? For the employer, your value can be as simple to calculate as how much you sell.

Have a think about what the three Whats mean to you? We will explore them more later.

What's the big idea?

We believe that career planning and development can be broken down into three clearly defined steps. These are:

- **Here & Now**. You need to know where you are starting from before you can set out in any given direction. Before you can really start to plan your development and future career direction, you *must* have a robust and accurate picture of exactly who you are, right *Here* and right *Now*.

- **There & Then**. Once you know who you are, you then need to think about what you want to achieve, who, what and where you want to be and what you want to be doing.

- **Bridge**. Once you know who you are, the Here & Now, and what you want to achieve, the There & Then, you can identify what you will need to do to be able to get you from one side of the Bridge to the other.

That's it. Simple. Common sense. Effective!

In this book we aim to take you through these steps, providing you with simple analysis exercises, tools and techniques to help guide you. It's not rocket science.

Reality check

If you choose to work through this book and use it to help you make a major change in your career or life, you must be aware that there will be something you have to give up, some price to pay, or some cost involved, and you must be prepared to accept it.

We'll look at this further in Chapter 4.

So, how does this book work?

For each of our three stages you will find an introductory section explaining what each means in more detail and discussing the issues arising from it. We will give you some true-life examples to demonstrate what we are telling you and we'll be asking you to ask yourself some key questions. Then, following each of these introductory sections, we will give you the tools to work through to help you on your way.

The tools we have chosen to include are designed to take no more than about 30 minutes to complete, but it may be that with some of them you choose to take more time. Take the Skills exercise in Chapter 4 for example, you may choose to complete it yourself initially, but then to test it by asking peers and colleagues to go through it with you. This would be a good thing to do – the more complete and robust the answers, the stronger the foundation upon which we can start to build the Bridge.

Similarly, in the section on There & Then tools (Chapter 6), the futurology tool is one that should be constantly updated, reflecting the constant changes in the environment. For example, an environmental scan exercise conducted before 11 September 2001 would have needed to be fundamentally reviewed since then. This applies to any change that affects not just the role and business in which we find ourselves but also the industry and the economy.

This book is a complete framework for career planning. It is only by working through the supporting tools, *and being entirely honest with yourself* in the process, that you will be able to make robust and effective decisions about your future. We cannot emphasize enough the need for honesty – look, it's quite simple; if you are reading this it's probably because you want to make a change in your career or life. Remembering that the majority of changes fail, you have to ask yourself how you can ensure that the change you want to make will be sustainable. It needs to be based on the facts, however painful, because otherwise you are talking about a dream, a career plan and a Bridge with foundations of sand.

The book has been laid out so that you will be able to refer back to it and update your planning as necessary, re-using the appropriate tools and helping you to re-evaluate where you are in the change you are making.

Successful people are successful because they love it, and they love it because they choose it. You can choose for yourself, right now, and be where you want to be.

'Learn nothing, and the next world is the same as this one, all the same limitations and lead weights to overcome.'

Richard Bach, *Jonathan Livingston Seagull*

chapter two
free agents

It's a free world

We live in an amazing time, for several reasons:

1 There are very few boundaries.

2 Communication between people is world-wide, constant and instant.

3 Individuals make a difference.

4 There is a talent war.

1 Boundaries

The close of the dot.com gold rush has taught everybody that what exists can face massive upheaval and that what is new and vibrant can be brought down by old-style economics. Yet the changes that occurred have ensured that we are aware that those things that we once perceived as boundaries no longer exist:

◆ Work will look like home and home will look like work. The difference between work and home is closing so that we can now choose a lifestyle that will combine both. Businesses have started asking themselves why they should pay exorbitant rates for office space when you have a perfectly good spare room in your own house, so work is invading people's homes. The 'payback' is that when you do go to the office, you now often have somewhere that you can go to relax, even just for a few minutes. So increasingly, businesses are finding that homes are invading the workplace too.

- The project you work on may be in another country, but you don't have to be there. Instead you get up and walk to your home office, sit in front of the camera and talk face to face with the local leader.

- You work for a local company whose products are global. A problem in one market is solved by data from another.

- Having finished your work day, you go home and work on your on-line business, liaising with like-minded entrepreneurs in six other countries to determine your market proposition and find funding.

Perceived boundaries of 18 months ago have disappeared. Many of our current boundaries will have vanished in the next 18 months. Wherever we look the walls are being broken down. We need to embrace these changes and use them to our advantage or we will get left behind. For free agents, they are opportunities or frontiers just waiting to be explored.

2 Communication

We can now talk without time or distance being an issue. The internet has put paid to that! I can e-mail you any time day or night, know you received the message and expect a reply instantly. Or you can always use a video phone, conferencing suite, a mobile phone or just talk on the telephone. There is no getting away from it: we live in a connected world.

3 Individuals make a difference

Knowledge is the most valuable resource any company has. It's been described by Charles Handy as 'tricky, as well as sticky and leaky'.

- **Tricky.** It can be difficult to pinpoint and define.

- **Sticky.** It stays in place and is difficult to move and transfer.

- **Leaky.** It walks out of the door of most companies at five o'clock.

Whilst business has invested in large information systems and more and more technological innovations, it is still often failing to address the fact that employees go home. *People make businesses work.* People have ideas, people get passionate. When was the last time you saw a passionate computer?

The contract is changing. Technology is the same from company to company: once one market leader has one system, you can bet if it gives them any advantage that all the others will also soon have it. That system was devised and designed by an individual who really owns it, who actually has it stored away inside them.

Microsoft, for example, is a large, technologically based company, and yet over 95% of the value of the business is tied up in the intellectual capital of the people who work there. Even at a company like British Petroleum (BP), the estimate is 75% intangible assets (i.e. in the heads of the employees). With all the knowledge-capture tools and techniques available to you, what do you think the percentage is in your business?

4   Talent wars

'You are only as good as your people, and the war for talent is intense.'

Thomas Weisel

If individuals contain your company's knowledge, their talent is your competitive advantage – so what does a company have to do to keep them? It can be summed up in three simple points:

◆ Protect and nurture the talent it has.

◆ Discover more talent.

◆ Poach other people's talent.

The advantage to you is that you are that talent, whether you like it or not, and the benefit to you is that the contract of work is changing and is swinging in your favour.

As companies have rightsized and downsized, removing complex and extensive hierarchies in the process, individuals have been empowered with more and more knowledge, information and influence. The individual can lever this knowledge and information to get what they want and need. The company has to begin to negotiate with the individual, because, at the end of the day, they can walk out of the building and away from the company, taking their knowledge, their experience, their skills, *their talent* with them.

What is a free agent?

So what does this mean for you as an individual? Here is a statement that may help make sense of it.

'The job is dead. No longer can we believe in having a piece of paper saying job description at the top. The new realities call for far greater flexibility. Throughout most of the twentieth century, managers averaged one job and one career. Now, we are talking about two careers and seven jobs. The days of the long-serving corporate man, safe and sound in the dusty recesses of the corporation, are long gone. Soon, the emphasis will be on getting a life instead of a career, and work will be viewed as a series of gigs or projects.

Inevitably, new roles demand new skills. Thirty years ago, we had to learn one new skill per year. Now, it is one new skill per day. Tomorrow, it may be one new skill per hour. Skills like networking – in 1960, the average manager had to learn 25 names throughout their entire career; today we must learn 25 new names every single month. Tomorrow, it may be 25 new names per week (and half of those are likely to be names from different languages).'

Jonas Ridderstrale and Kjell Nordstrom, Funky Business

Historically, individual career histories were defined as having ten stages, as shown in Figure 2.1.

Figure 2.1 *Major stages of a career*

Source: Edgar H. Schien, *Career Anchors: Discovering Your Real Values*, Jossey-Bass, Pfeiffer, 1990

Yet, given the *Funky Business* statement, and what we know about the free world, what does a career look like now and in the future? We can assume that for most the stages given above will still exist.

However, in the free agent world we may never gain membership of the area in which we first enter, but, instead, may move to other areas where we can still use our initial education and training. Once there, we will set about gaining additional skills and expertise that can either be used within this new environment, or later be used to enter another area. In effect we are constantly moving between levels 4 and 5 and, by so doing, we have become 'free agents'. As a 'free agent':

- We initialize and gain membership in associated or non-associated areas.

- We move between periods of re-education, skill enhancement and leveraging skills for reward.

- The expectations for reward change as we expect to take care of ourselves instead of relying on an employer or employing organization.

- As one door closes, we work to open another through networking, reputation and results.

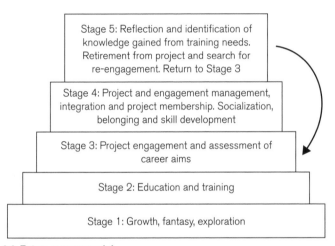

Figure 2.2 *Future career model*

Figure 2.1 can be adapted for free agents so that the careers histories and changes are less hierarchical (Figure 2.2).

So being a free agent means ownership and responsibility. It means recognizing that you, as an individual, have a brand. That you are effectively a business in your own right and that, as such, you *have* to invest in yourself if you are to succeed. No business ever became a market leader by standing still. You need to be constantly aware of and working to enhance your own *reputation, development and self-marketing*. You plc!

So what does it mean to be a free agent?

If you accept that it is becoming a free agent's world out there, what happens if you work in a large corporation?

The same things matter of course.

Consider the following rules for a free agent:

1 When times get tough it's quality that counts.

2 Free to be you and me.

3 You are on the line.

4 Promotion is not the only direction.

5 Bigger is not better. Better is better.

6 Forget survival of the fittest, we need one another.

These rules were proposed in Daniel H. Pink's *Free Agent Nation: How America's New Independent Workers Are Transforming the Way We Live*. What do they mean?

1   When times get tough it's quality that counts

It is not how hard you work, it is how smart you work and how you present what you do. It is Your brand, whether it is inside a corporation or not. Don't forget that you are looking after your own professional reputation as well as that of the business you work for.

2   Free to be you and me

If you are not being true to yourself, who are you living your life for? Within business there is no time for you to pretend to be who you are not. If you are, you are being false and this may be the reason why you may not be getting anywhere. In the free agent world you are free to be who you are. What is so different in the corporate world? If they don't take you for who you are, why are you there?

'Some people will like me and some won't. So I might as well be myself and then at least I'll know that the people who like me, like *me*.'

Hugh Prather

3 You are on the line

If free agency is living on the edge, what is so different in a corporation? With quarterly reviews, annual development plans, balanced scorecards and being only as good as your last review, what is so different? Where is the job security?

4 Promotion is not the only direction

Corporations are now so flat in structure terms that promotion is often not an option. Do you train for a job that may never materialize (and in today's constant downsizing, upsizing and resizing, promotional positions are often rightsized out of existence)? Do you sit tight and wait in the hope that you might be asked to fill a dead man's shoes, if and when your boss moves on? Do you accept that for development and skill enhancement, sideways is often the only way to go? Do you change direction completely, even if it means taking a short-term backward/downward step?

Don't assume that your long-term development can only be achieved by climbing the corporate ladder.

5 Bigger is not better. Better is better

So you get to a high corporate level – are they winning or are you? If the business gives you a smart computer, a big salary with bigger bonus and a flashy car, what do they expect in return – what is the price you pay? Are you now expected to spend all week away from home as a road warrior, working long hours, staying in average-to-poor hotels, never seeing your family, not having time to pursue other interests and spending weekends recovering before starting all over again on Monday morning? Worse still, are you expected to keep your colleagues on their toes by being a bastard so that you can get ahead?

'The things you own end up owning you.'

Brad Pitt, *Fight Club*

A bigger job means bigger responsibility and bigger pressure. You need to understand what level of responsibility and pressure you want and position yourself accordingly. What else is going on in your life, and what are your priorities? Is getting the 'bigger' job really better for you?

6   Forget survival of the fittest, we need one another

With constant change and reorganization, it's the people who are connected who win. They network, they talk to people to find out what's going on. In the free agent world you do it to help one another, to market yourself, to demonstrate that you are motivated and to make best use of those around you. This also helps during periods of recession. It is those who are connected who survive and find work even when the going is tough.

The skills you need to succeed in the free agent world are the same as those needed in the corporate world. The only difference is that in the free agent world they are used to manage *your own, personal brand, growth and self-worth*. As the talent war starts, the skills will not change – it's the same game, but you need to re-assess how you are using them and what for. You can still be a self-proclaimed free agent within the corporate world. Only now you are using your skills for your own maximum benefit and not just for the good of the corporation.

Similarly, during the internet boom, this idea of being a flexible worker was christened the '*Unit of One*' by *Fast Company* magazine. The 'Unit of One' is subject to certain rules:

◆ As an individual you are only as good as your last result.

◆ Have a unique set of skills and talents that can enable you to go anywhere you want.

- By combining your talents with those of others (networking), small and, in some cases, large teams can be formed that are better than the sum of the individual parts.

- All work is made up of a series of projects or engagements that have pre-defined success criteria for the customer.

- It is up to you to maintain and improve the skills you have.

- Only you can determine what you want from life, particularly if you want to take part in the decision-making process.

- You may determine your own reward based on what you want to accomplish: money, power, service to others, compassion, pressure or less pressure.

Think about this in relation to your own position.

How do I become a free agent?

As a free agent you have to do a lot of things for yourself. The following list will give you some food for thought of what's needed:

- Periods of reskilling replacing unemployment.

- Information technology skills with common software programs.

- The ability to master changes in information technology and master new technology.

- Good communication skills: listening, questioning, presenting, writing, assertiveness, influencing, negotiation, coaching and mentoring.

- Time management.

- Ability to adopt socialization and specialization approaches, depending on which is most appropriate.

- Project management.

- Problem-solving, including being open-minded.

- Strong networking skills.

- Decision-making ability based on limited company knowledge.

- Sales skills: selling what you do, your ideas and achievements.

- Fee-orientated work – based on time, quality, reputation and reliability.

- Clients not bosses.

- Fees based on the knowledge that can be applied without being constrained by pay scales.

Most important of all is environmental awareness. You have to be constantly checking what is going on around you, not just within your team or business or industry but also in the wider economy, the global markets and in the job markets. All the skills and training in the world are useless unless they can be applied and managed in the current environment.

Scanning Appointments pages, and looking at how large companies are now approaching recruitment and staffing issues, will give you clear indications of trends and management approaches which are likely to affect you in the future. For example, we have seen a sharp increase in recent years in the number of employers offering fixed-term contracts. There is far greater emphasis being placed on the individual to take responsibility for ensuring that they are 'current' in whatever area of expertise they place themselves in. We may see a company advertising for a Project Manager to work in a very specific area for a one-year contract. Why?

- The company gets to pick from a range of trained Project Managers, knowing that each individual will arrive with up-to-date skills appropriate to the work that needs doing and appropriate to their system needs, i.e. no start-up training is required.

- The company knows that during the course of the next 12 months the Project Manager will deliver skills and expertise that do not currently exist within the company. This gives the individual selected experience within a new environment and offers the company the opportunity to learn from an expert.

◆ The company has no responsibility for training the Project Manager. Whilst working on the fixed contract for the business, the Project Manager must organize and pay for their own training if they are to develop, to be positioned to be able to renew the contract or to move on to another engagement with other clients.

◆ The business knows that, in a year's time, it can again advertise for another Project Manager or retain the current manager without having to worry about redundancy, severance or constructive dismissal packages. If the individual has not made the effort to keep themselves 'current', the company is perfectly placed to end the contract and bring in someone else. The same applies if the individual has not fitted in socially/personally.

◆ The company does not need to worry about many of the personnel-related obligations that may arise if the manager were on a permanent contract (e.g. maternity/paternity leave, sick leave, etc.).

This might sound like doom and gloom, but it isn't. For the free agent who is aware and prepared for the possibility that this will happen, both inside and outside companies, there is a world of opportunity out there – a chance to go and experience and learn from a wide variety of companies, in different environments and cultures. Most importantly this can be the perfect opportunity to choose and shape the direction in which your career takes you.

Let's look at the arguments listed above from the free agent's point of view:

◆ The free agent gets to choose which companies they work for, what types of projects they work on and whether they wish to specialize in any given area.

◆ The free agent is in a position of strength as the resident 'expert' within the company. The individual decides how much/many of their skills and knowledge they impart to the company.

- The free agent decides on their own development needs, the most appropriate development format and time-scales, and is able to select an intervention most appropriate to their own long-term needs and goals, rather than reflecting the specific needs of any given company or industry.

- The free agent knows that in a year's time they can decide not to negotiate a new contract and instead to move away to work with another company, or even to try working in a different area. There is no long-term loyalty to the company which offers a fixed-term contract.

- The free agent is aware enough of the risks involved in entering into a fixed-term contract with a company to be able to manage it accordingly – either by ensuring that appropriate clauses are included in any contract, or by making suitable provision of their own to manage any situations which may arise.

Food for thought.

chapter three
here & now

How can you move until you know where you're starting from?

We want you to start by thinking hard about your current place in the world (close your eyes if it helps). What is your job? What do you do socially? Who are your friends and what does your family look like? If we were to visit your life, what would it look like?

And then think about why.

We'll come back to this in a minute. The truth is that the majority of us think about career planning stuff purely in relation to our work, so let's start by looking at that.

The vast majority of us start in employment after school or university and are swept up in the role, the business and the people with whom we work. Very often the job we go into is not necessarily anything that we had ever thought of doing, but it just follows on from our qualifications, or is handy because we're introduced to it by a friend. As time passes we either carry on in the same business, or progress within the same field, never really stopping to consider why we made our choice, or even that we had one. Then comes a sudden realization from somewhere deep in our subconscious mind that we really don't want to be here, we want to be doing something else. And what do we do about it? Some people do nothing: they continue with the status quo. Some people don't even think about it: they just jump ship and do something radically different on a whim. Some jump ship straight into something that they have always wanted to do. Some people buy a book or enrol on a course looking for inspired intervention.

Ralph's story

Ralph was a successful Broker working in London's money markets, but after eight years of (very) early mornings and being constantly stressed by knowing that one mistake would cost him his job, he had had enough. Through his contacts in the City he was invited to join a small start-up company and to become a stakeholder, therefore guaranteeing him job security and a role in helping to build the company. Ralph bought a big house in an expensive area of the commuter belt and felt generally happier with his life, but there were still doubts.

Two years later, the doubts and nagging frustration persisted, so Ralph decided to take things into his own hands. He resigned and enrolled at university to do a three-year course in Physiology. He had saved enough money to be able to complete the course without working and build up only a small debt in the process. At the end of the course he did not know what he would do for a living, he had no job lined up, but despite that, for the first time in over ten years, he felt that he was genuinely doing something that he wanted to do.

Ralph is on the course as we write this book. He is still very happy and confident that he will be okay when the course finishes. The important thing for Ralph is that he made the decision himself, aware of the risks and the price he would have to pay for making such a radical change. He chose his course of action and has total ownership of his own destiny now, for better or for worse.

So why have you bought this book?

Possibly you feel a nagging sense of discontent or are vaguely unhappy with your lot? Perhaps you realize that you cannot keep doing what you are doing, knowing that there are things you want to do that remain unfulfilled? Perhaps you need some advice or an idea of what to do next?

When you start a new job the world of work is like the merry-go-round with a fire engine on it that you rode as a child. When you got on the ride you'd be eagerly ringing the bell and turning the wheel, making it all come alive. With time, age and experience you find yourself in a position where you are able to step back and look at what really happens. The fire engine is located on a stage that is controlled by an operator. The operator decides when to start the merry-go-round, what speed it goes round, the length of the ride and when to stop it. The ride loses its appeal – and that is what happens to people in work every day!

We get up, we go to work and we ring that bell for all we are worth. We follow the processes, we attend the meetings and we fill in the forms. What a fantastic ride! Until the day that we step back from the merry-go-round and we have a look at what's happening. Then we have a choice: do we go back and climb onto the ride and carry on ringing the bell, or do we step off? If we step off, we can go back to a similar ride, or we can try a different ride, and maybe this time we might want to decide when to start the ride, when to stop the ride and how fast it goes whilst we are on it. Is that why you're here?

Reality check

So why did we ask you to close your eyes and think about things like your family, your friends and your social life? Because before you decide to try a different ride you need to be thinking about all these other things – they are all connected through you. Change something fundamental, like your job, and it could have repercussions on all other aspects of your life. So, from this point, start thinking much wider than just about your job – think about your whole life, everyone and everything in it.

It's time to be a free agent in your world of choice!

You can't just easily step from driving the fire engine to controlling the merry-go-round. Just because you know something is wrong does not mean you can fix it easily and quickly. First you need to sort out where you are *Here & Now*. You will need to do some reflection on where you are, where you have been, what your skills and strengths are, what you enjoy doing, etc., and then, and only then, can you look at where you want to go and how to get there. Yes, you could jump a few steps, but you may find that later on you are still unhappy at the direction you're heading in because you have made decisions on incomplete information.

When you begin a journey of any sort you need to have a starting point from which to plan: a location, an idea of what you want to do, how long you want to be away, and so on. You now need to try to understand the point from which you will make your first step in your career change. As Confucius once said,

'A journey starts with the first step.'

This is one of those blindingly obvious statements used in business all the time. Your first step will be some self-analysis – not too detailed, but strategic and high-level. Now stop, take a minute and make sure that you're not feeling overly cynical.

If you're feeling a bit sceptical and cynical, you need to put that to one side for the moment. We are trying to be honest here and it is hard. It's hard to tell people that they need to learn from their past in order to move forward successfully – it sounds like a cliché, but it's the truth. It's only by looking at the past and where it has brought you that you can decide what went right, what went wrong, what needs changing and what to do about it. By getting this stage right you can start to choose your choice, make decisions based on *your* needs and future requirements and not leave them in the hands of others.

The Here & Now is your starting point. It's where you are today and where you'll take your first step from. We could say to you, 'Okay, so you want to be in Marketing. Just do this …' – but this wouldn't work. We believe that before you even think about where you want to go and how fast you want to get there (There & Then), you have to understand who you are now and what has brought you to this point. If you don't, chances are you will either miss something very important or waste time and effort trying to learn something that you already know.

Where are you now?

Are you the person you expected to be at this stage in your career?

We have asked ourselves the same question many times, and each time the answer has been 'no'. Neither of us expected to be working for the company we are, nor did we expect to find ourselves in the positions we are now. We are typical of most people, people who have been swept up in the work environment and been prepared to join the ranks of the corporate masses. Until we started working with people on career development issues, we failed to think about who we were, who we wanted to be and what we wanted from a career.

How does that happen? It just does. Time is speeding up, business is moving to a faster and faster beat. How many of us feel that we are able to take the time to stop and think about what we are doing, where we are going and how come we have managed to forget our dreams?

We all get so caught up with what is happening at home, at work and everywhere else in our lives that we just concentrate on contending with difficulties and developing strategies to cope. By just coping, we withdraw from our dreams and goals, and by the time we wake up to our situation, we have sometimes missed our best opportunities.

What can you do about it?

You need to step back, stop ringing that fire engine bell and act like a captain who has run his ship aground. Walk around the deck and take a good look at what is happening. Take a look at:

◆ who you are;

◆ what you are doing;

◆ what you have done that has brought you to this point;

- what you have learned along the way;

- what's become important to you;

- where you would like to be.

Our aim is to help you to understand yourself better, appreciate your own viewpoint and where it comes from, and then to be better able to understand how others perceive you. You need to have all these things clear and at the forefront of your mind in order to aid development. We want to create a 'snapshot', a freeze frame in your life's cinematic progress. The picture created will fade over time and will need re-taking. The aim is to take the picture regularly: use it, re-touch it, alter the background and move forward. However, *a word of caution*: you are setting out to change things in your life and the problem with change is – *Nobody likes it!* It upsets people and causes anger and frustration. Yet the fact is that change is the one true constant that we all have to deal with.

Can you deal with change?

When we're dealing with a change of any sort it's generally accepted that we all go through the same stages and our emotions all follow the same pattern. The difference is that some of us do it quickly and some of us go through it very slowly.

The Change Loop (see Figure 3.1) affects us all as we go through any change. In turn we face the following stages:

- **Denial.** We are uncomfortable with change and think that by ignoring it, it will not happen.

- **Defence.** We take actions that we hope will prevent change, or we try to position ourselves so that the change will not affect us.

- **Discard.** When the change is acknowledged, we try to argue against it or refuse to use it, preferring instead to keep to the

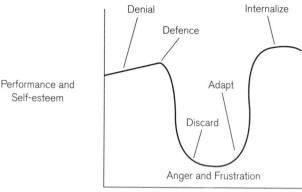

Figure 3.1 *The Change Loop*

'good old ways' in the hope and expectation that the change will go away.

◆ **Anger and frustration.** We find that the change has happened and we rage against the system, ourselves and anybody who is near before we finally accept that we have to discard the old system and adapt to the new.

◆ **Adapt.** We accept that the change has happened, explore the implications, what has happened, what is happening and its effect on us.

◆ **Internalize.** We have adapted to change, accepted it as the new norm and move forward.

You will get to anger and frustration. Accept the inevitable – because it affects us emotionally: *change hurts!*

Karen's story

The company Karen was working for decided that it made economic sense to move from a cramped and expensive office block in an unattractive and dirty part of central London to a spacious office suite near Reading, overlooking a beautiful park, saving about 30% of the current rent in the process. Changing a 15-minute commute for Karen into a journey of upwards of an hour and a half.

The problem for Karen was that she did not want to move office. She loved the company, her job and the people and she couldn't imagine working with or for anyone else, but she didn't want to move office. Why? Because Karen and her partner had just finished redecorating the house they owned in North London. They had bought the house together when it was run down and had slaved for the last two years decorating it to get it looking just right. The house was perfectly located for the office, was only about half a mile from the park, was a good-size home in which to start a family (something Karen was considering) and was just as she wanted it. She liked the situation she was in and felt that she had control of her life.

So how did she react when it was decided that the move would go ahead?

◆ **Denial.** 'The company move? Won't happen. We're perfectly positioned here for our clients so they will realize that it makes far more sense for us to stay here.'

◆ **Defence.** 'But can't they see that it will be impossible for me to commute out to Reading? I have an important role here: I am leading on four key accounts at the moment, two of which are located near here. Surely they must see how this is going to disrupt my work. If this goes ahead I won't be able to do my job effectively and they will end up with me being really demotivated. I think that I should start looking for other jobs that'll allow me to stay closer to home. Once they realize that I might be going they might change their tack.'

◆ **Discard.** Karen refused to pack her own files and equipment into boxes for the move; in fact, she refused to help with the move at all. She even refused to visit the new site until the company actually opened for business in the new offices and she had to be there to work.

- **Anger and frustration.** Karen started doing, or not doing, things to undermine her personal performance, and therefore that of the business, and blaming it on the move/change (e.g. turning up late, deliberately, for meetings and blaming it on the problems of commuting back and forth between Reading and North London). 'I told you that it was a ridiculous idea moving all the way out here!'

- **Adapt.** It took some time for Karen to get her head out of the sand and start to look around at her new work surroundings. The thing was that she did still love her job and the company, it was just the commute she hated. After working in the offices for a couple of months she was invited to have lunch in the park with some colleagues and really enjoyed it. She started to look around the area to see what it was like and found that she quite liked it.

- **Internalize.** After working there for a number of months Karen realized that she really did not want to work for any other company. She discussed the situation with her partner and they agreed to consider options for where they could live that would be suitable for both their needs. They would be disappointed to leave the house in North London, but recognized that the work that they had done had added greatly to the value of the property, so they might be able to find somewhere even better which would make Karen's commute more manageable.

At the time of writing, Karen is still house hunting – we hope that by the time of publication she has found somewhere suitable!

When we go through change it can sometimes take us a long time to get through the Change Loop, and it takes support and understanding to get through it without being scarred by the experience. The problem with this is that:

Time + Association + Support + Understanding = Massive Investment

Yes, there is a cost to making a change. If you are reading this book because you want to make a change in your life, be prepared for the fact that an emotional investment is involved.

Your job in this book is to find a direction for the future and a route to get there. But before you can do that, you need to take a look back to see what has brought you to this point. There will be things that you will want to discard, and long-forgotten things that you will want to restore and keep. It will take both time and effort. But the more you can invest, the quicker you can get through the loop and the sooner you can move forward. Don't reflect too heavily on anything that has happened – it's in the past and the past's often the best place to leave it. Once you are done, turn away and look to the future instead. Use this book to help you identify what changes, if any, you need to make, and then look to manage those changes as effectively as you can to create maximum value for yourself, whilst not lapsing back to where you were before.

What do you do next?

In the next chapter we'll give you some exercises to help you reflect on who you are and what you are doing. You might have seen some of them before as we have taken things that work from any area we can. Hey, what works, works! Alternatively, you can use this chapter as preparation for your annual appraisal. It should enable you to reflect very quickly on the past year and go into a meeting understanding what has happened, what you have achieved and what you have learned. Given the speed of today, anything that enables you to complete a task quickly and gain insight at the same time can't be bad, can it?

We favour short and sharp exercises that take a maximum of 20 to 30 minutes. Also don't focus on trying to get them all done at once – BORING! Aim to fit one in every now and again – they don't have to be completed in one sitting. We must also point out that these are aimed at you as a work brand, focusing on your skills and attributes in the work environment – and remember to be honest!

So, we are starting by creating your Here & Now; then we will look ahead to the finish point, your There & Then. Then we will help you build the Bridge between the two. Let's do it!

04

chapter four
tools – get thinking

Here & Now tools

In this chapter we are going to start you on the way to working out exactly who You are by offering you some tools to get you thinking. These are by no means the only tools that you can use to do this and indeed we would encourage you to look at other sources, and choose those that most suit you. We have selected tools that will cover each of what we consider to be the four main areas for consideration when going about this type of analysis:

◆ What skills and capabilities do you have?

◆ What are your values and priorities?

◆ How are you perceived by others?

◆ What's going on around you, and how does it impact on you?

Whatever tools you choose to use, you *must* ensure that you cover all of these areas.

We have divided Here & Now tools into four parts, each reflecting one of these areas, and we have included a section entitled 'Your Notes' at the end of each tool in which you can scribble. Now it's up to you.

Important note

These tools should not be used once and then forgotten. You plc is a complex, constantly evolving entity, changing and developing just as fast as everything else in the world. These tools are re-useable. So go ahead – make the most of them!

Who are you?

Very few of us are fully aware of who and what we are. The pace of the day rushes us ever onwards and we fail to sit down and work out who we are, what we believe in, what we enjoy, what motivates us and (and every bit as important) what we detest. We just let it all get thrown at us and we cope. Why is it that the people who are happy and have got where they want to be are so confident? It's because they know what they want, know who they are and focus on the mission they have set for themselves. So if we want to be our own Career Consultant, one of the first things we need to know is who we are.

So how do we find out who we are? Let's make a start.

What can you do about it?

What skills and capabilities do you have? What can you bring to the career party (bar a big bottle)? You need to identify what current skills, abilities and competencies you have.

◆ A **skill** is: a special ability or expertise, a trade or expertise, often acquired by training.

◆ An **ability** is: the possession of a necessary skill or power to be able to do something.

◆ A **competence** is: a capacity or power, but one you might not be experienced in using at the present time.

Here's a list of some skills, abilities and competencies. It's not comprehensive, but it's a good starter:

- **Achieving.** Identifying risks, and taking responsibility for actions. Gaining acceptance of and commitment to those actions.

- **Administering.** Managing or overseeing.

- **Advising.** Recommending a course of action.

- **Analyzing.** Distinguishing the significant elements of a situation.

- **Assembling.** Managing or overseeing.

- **Budgeting.** Estimating the amount of money needed or available for a situation.

- **Calculating.** Ascertaining mathematical problems.

- **Caring.** Expressing feelings of concern or interest.

- **Classifying.** Assigning categories to a person, place or object.

- **Clerical.** Copying, entering and record-keeping skills.

- **Communicating: (a) written; (b) oral.** Conveying and receiving information.

- **Computing.** Reckoning, generally with the use of high-tech equipment.

- **Construction/building.** The skill of putting something together by following a plan of instructions.

- **Controlling.** Setting up monitoring systems and taking corrective action where necessary.

- **Counselling and coaching.** Helping a person improve their performance by defining problems and gaining their commitment to action.

- **Decision-making.** Establishing the purpose of a decision; evaluating and selecting a course of action that satisfies the decision and carries least risk.

- **Delegating.** Handing over work to a subordinate or peer in such a way that the person has the necessary guidelines and commitment to complete the task correctly.

- **Designing.** Creating a plan for a purpose or objective.

- **Developing.** Creating progress.

- **Diagnosing.** Ascertaining the cause of malfunctions.

- **Editing.** Able to review material and reassess content in order to reduce volume but maintain essence.

- **Evaluating.** Considering objectively how well each alternative meets objectives and what the risk areas are.

- **Flexibility.** Seeing yourself in relation to others and as others see you in different situations.

- **Generating alternatives.** Creating a number of options to improve or overcome a situation.

- **Identifying priorities.** Assessing the comparative level of importance of tasks.

- **Information extraction.** Tracing or retrieving given facts or data.

- **Innovating.** Making changes or creating new solutions.

- **Instructing.** Making known to a person what he or she is required to do.

- **Managing and supervising.** Having executive control or authority.

- **Mechanical dexterity.** Ability to work with machinery.

- **Memorizing.** Remembering and recalling given pieces of information or facts.

- **Motivating.** Generating a willingness to work.

- **Negotiating.** Persuading and bargaining to get agreement and commitment.

- **Numerical.** Working effectively with numbers.

- **Observing.** Watching and examining situations, people and trends.

- **Organizing.** Structuring, arranging and allocating resources so that they are effectively utilized.

- **Persuading.** Inducing another towards your inclination.

- **Planning.** Identifying the key tasks to be completed.

- **Problem-solving.** Overcoming difficult questions or tasks.

- **Researching.** Discovering or collating old facts.

- **Responsibility-taking.** The willingness to assume levels of authority and responsibility to achieve desired results.

- **Risk-taking or speculating.** The combination of initiative and judgement that together display a willingness to opt for great profits but high-risk probability.

- **Surveying.** Inspecting or investigating the condition or amount of a given subject.

- **Teaching.** Enabling a person to gain knowledge through instruction.

- **Training.** Bringing someone to a desired standard of efficiency.

- **Using intuition.** Attaining immediate insight without the use of reasoning.

- **Validating.** Establishing the truth of a situation by testing against reality.

Add any skills, abilities and competencies that you feel are missing, including any that you regard as hobbies.

EXERCISE

Now take a sheet of paper and list what you regard as your own skills, abilities and competencies.

At this stage don't filter anything that you have or are able to put down on paper. Just let it flow. Often one statement, word or phrase opens up numerous others. Take no more than 20 minutes to do this and then sit back and reflect.

Think about the skills in terms of:

◆ I can …

◆ I have the ability to …

◆ If required I can …

Now we need to order them. The critical decision to be taken here is: can I transfer this skill or ability and repeat it in another area or business? Or is it specific to a single area of business and industry?

EXERCISE *continued*

Use two sheets of paper, or draw up a table like the one we have used below. Transfer the statements you have made into one of the two categories. For example:

Transferable	*Specific*
I am great at presenting.	I am good at using MS Project software.
I am sociable and personable.	I can run a project or programme using PRINCE project management methodology.
I can adapt quickly to changing situations.	I can apply the 7 Cs of Consulting in engaging with a client.
I can see how new products and projects fit into the strategic needs of the business.	I am great at preparing a business for Investor in People accreditation.
I am great at making complicated issues simple and easy to understand.	

The reason for separating the generic (transferable) skills and the specific skills is that the generic skills and abilities give you a strong base of skills on which to build. Structured and used correctly, they can give you a lot more options. They can liberate you from one industry or role and enable you to take a much wider view – to look at any industry as an option for the future or, if you choose, to consider becoming a free agent.

Specific, technical or specialist skills can be advantageous if your values and career anchor (see pages 54–59) point towards mastery and speciality, particularly if you know that you want to stay in that area. What you may be looking for is that promotion or added responsibility that will bring with it a better package (more money) and/or an increased status or reputation. However, for many this is not the case, and in the future it will be increasingly important to have transferable skills that adapt more easily as industries stand still for less and less time. These skills form the 'bottom line' of what You plc has to offer.

We want to avoid limiting our horizons and becoming job-specific. In the free agent world it's our ability to be able to compete in many skill areas that will assure our employability. Similarly in the corporate world, what was once a job specifically involving marketing may now involve business plan writing, resource allocation and project planning, amongst any number of other skills. Our ability to apply a combination of skills enhances our corporate employability as well as our opportunities as a free agent.

As we've mentioned, Here & Now is where we're starting from, what this side of the Bridge looks like. Once we've decided where we want to go, this skill set forms the foundations of the Bridge to make the change sustainable. We can also then see what skills we need to work on to enable us to get there.

Reality check

But you shouldn't necessarily believe what you have put down on your list
– *go and check it! Ask others for their opinion.* We are almost all guilty of
sabotaging ourselves when it comes to identifying our own skill set, our
own strengths and weaknesses. We have to be honest with ourselves. If
we are not, we are only lying to ourselves. Be brave! Go and ask someone
whom you trust to be honest and objective with you to look at your list
and tell you what they think – *honestly.*

Sometimes this can hurt or sometimes it can be tremendously uplifting
and rewarding to start to recognize what other people see as your
strengths. But whichever way it goes, you need the list to be accurate if
you are to build your Bridge on solid foundations.

YOUR NOTES

What are your values?

Our values make us what we are. They have been built into us throughout our lives, influenced at different times by our parents, by school, college and/or university, by our life experiences as well as by the jobs/roles that we have had, with all their differing levels of responsibility and challenge. You need to understand what your values are because they act as your internal rudders, guiding you. They impact on everything you do.

What might you consider as your values? Here is a list that we have drawn up to start you thinking about it:

Adventure	Artistic	Challenge	Choice	Competition
Completing	Contact	Creativity	Distinction	Excitement
Fame	Family	Fast pace	Fortune	Friendship
Funky	Growth	Helping	Independence	Integrity
Involvement	Money	Mastery	Morality	Passion
Power	Pressure	Prestige	Promotion	Loyalty
Respect	Risk	Routine	Self-esteem	Status
Success	Surroundings	Time	Variety	Learning
Rapport	Honesty	Quality	Privacy	Peace
Balance	Excellence	Co-operation	Reward	Recognition
Politics	Community	Trust	Justice	Security

By identifying which values we feel passionately about, we can:

◆ start to identify what is important to us;

◆ start to define industries/companies/areas/jobs/roles that will
attract us by sharing these values and enabling us to live them;

◆ identify those values that we want to avoid and so define areas of
work we want to avoid.

This is important because our values are represented in our inherent
behaviours. They are about the way we choose to live our lives and
the subconscious rules by which we govern ourselves. Values are not
about *what we say*, they are about *what we do*. It follows, therefore,
that if you work somewhere where the values they expect you to
demonstrate are different to your own, *you will **not** be happy there!*

For example, if you are inherently honest, cannot tell lies, would
always tell the truth whatever the consequences, then you should
have honesty in your list of top five values.

EXERCISE

Try now to identify the top five values that are important to you and
those that you must avoid and list them. You should end up with
something like the table given below.

Most important	*Avoid*
Creativity	Routine
Funky	Pressure
Variety	Well-known employer
Recognition	Staid – environment and people
Time – development	Solitude

Take some time to reflect on what you have written. Can you identify
the values that you have chosen for yourself? Think of times that

work and assignments went well. Did these instances have a good values match with yourself? Think of times when things were bad! Were these times when your values were being eroded and abused?

The idea is that the values that are important to you should give you an indication of the type of work that may be of interest to you. You can use them to help define the sort of role that is most appropriate for you. We call this, defining our *career anchor*.

So what is your career anchor?

Edgar H. Schien completed lots of work on career theory. His work indicated that all people have a career anchor based on their values and listed eight specific career anchors (see his *Career Anchors*). He also indicated that by knowing your career anchor, you would be better able to find a match between your work and your personality.

Here's a synopsis of the eight career anchors he identified. Compare your values to the eight career anchors – highlight what you recognize in yourself – and see where there are matches:

1   **Technical/function competence.** These are people who have a strong skill in one particular area and are less inclined towards general management. They enjoy the exercising of their skill and the recognition it can bring from their peers. They enjoy a sense of worth from being around similarly skilled people and skill-orientated groups (professional membership). Work is defined for them by the challenge and the application of their skill. They are often goal-orientated and perfectionist when completing a task and demanding when budgets or resources may not be to their satisfaction. They often lack general competence and people skills, and find that a career to more senior levels can be difficult when not aligned to their needs. However, advancement for the individual may not be power-focused but aimed at further skill development, specialization and challenge.

2 **General managerial competence.** These people have a range of competencies and recognize in themselves this need. They enjoy moving up the ladder to higher levels of responsibility and are highly motivated. They are proficient in and enjoy solving challenges with incomplete data and high levels of uncertainty by stating the challenges in such a way that decisions can be made. As well as high analytical abilities, they have high interpersonal and people skills, giving them the ability to influence and control people towards goal achievement. By bringing people together they solve problems and are stimulated by that responsibility. They rely on needing the large competency set and having challenging, varied and integrative work. By measuring work by its importance and failure as defeat, they expect high remuneration, are bonus-orientated and expect to get promotion when achieving results.

3 **Autonomy.** These people do not want to be bound by rules, processes and codes. They need to do things their way, at their pace and to their own standards. They will often follow a career that is according to their own needs and they need to feel that they are managing themselves. Thus they tend towards autonomous business or a tendency to work remotely from both a people and a geographic perspective. Once they have been given a goal they wish to be left alone to complete it. Compensation therefore represents mixed and matched options to their needs without any strings attached. Promotion should result in more not less independence. Recognition by testament and awards are preferred more than promotion and rank increase.

4 **Security.** These people require a safe and secure career with the future being reasonably predictable. They seek companies and positions that offer long-term stability and often have good retirement plans. Willing to give up career management to their employers, they are happy to be told what to do and can be perceived as lacking ambition. They can reach high levels in organizations but challenge and enrichment mean less than pay and conditions. Rewards and promotion are preferred based on length of service and a grade system that pays attention to loyalty

over time. Often these people are attracted by Government and Civil Service orientated organizations.

5 **Entrepreneurial creativity.** These people feel the need to develop new products, services or businesses where money is the high-level measure of success. Their creative urge is driven by the need to be identified and rewarded for their efforts and the need to prove themselves. Highly motivated, these people find it difficult to stay in traditional industries and get bored easily when unable to be creative. They move between roles depending on what needs they have and enjoy publicity and public recognition. Wealth shows what they have created, and often their personality and companies are very representative of themselves.

6 **Service/dedication.** Motivated by the need to serve, these people desire to improve the world in some way. Often they tend towards general management and work in areas that allow them to influence the organization and its policies in the direction of their values. Reward must be fair but is not the overriding factor. These people would exchange this for authority that allows them more influence and the ability to use it. They need to feel that others share their values and that they are recognized by their peers and superiors because of these values.

7 **Challenge.** If the impossible exists, these people must solve it, beating others in the process and driven by the need to win. The tougher and more complex the problem, the more achievement they feel. It does not matter in what area of competence the challenge exists, only that it needs to be solved. Therefore, they require roles that constantly challenge them and in which they do not become bored. They need variety and at times steep learning curves to stay on top of their game. Highly motivated, without challenge they can be difficult and complex to manage. Particularly if they are in a non-competitive environment they can become demoralized and a problem to themselves and others.

8 **Lifestyle.** These are people who are committed to a career but need that career to also fit in with their total lifestyle. This means that they wish to balance their career with their family and their individuality. These are people who want flexibility so that as

their needs change so can and do their career aims, and so must the options offered by the organization. Remuneration is thus not an issue, more that the organization must have an attitude that allows them the integration and holistic management of their life and its needs at any given time.

Go back over the career anchors and read them again if necessary. Can you see yourself in any one anchor? If you can, make a note of it with your important values and values to avoid. It may also be that you see yourself in two of the anchors. However, *decide on one primary anchor* and the other as a secondary anchor. Intuition will tell you which is the primary anchor.

Now perhaps, by having your values and an understanding of your primary career anchor, you can test out where you are now. Map what you believe to be the values and anchor of the company you are working for or the engagement team you are working with at the moment. Do they match your own?

If you want to, go further back and consider all the companies you have worked for and your superiors within them. What does the comparison show? In the free agent world you have the opportunity to use this to help you to decide who you want to work for. In the corporate world this test can be used to see whether you match the ideal of the company you work for or a company you have applied to.

Matt's story

Matt worked for a public relations company in London and he had become increasingly frustrated with his slow progress through the business. He felt that others had been promoted ahead of him, been given bigger, more attractive accounts to manage and were leaving him with the feeling of being 'passed over'. His disillusionment led him to start looking for jobs elsewhere, not only within the world of public relations but in other sectors as well.

Through a friend, Matt was introduced to a senior partner of a financial management company in the City and, over a friendly beer, made enough of an impression to be invited for an interview. Matt went along, feeling quite enthused and excited, but this feeling disappeared when he walked through the door and into the reception of the company he was visiting.

Matt was used to a work environment that was lively, often noisy, exciting, relied heavily on strong inter-personal skills and where good dress sense had been a cultural necessity. All of this had made the day-to-day work of managing accounts seem like fun. So Matt was horrified to find himself now sitting in a large open-plan office with a dark grey carpet, black desks and chairs and everyone in the room wearing the same 'uniform' – a dark grey suit, white shirt, black shoes and a dark tie. It was like being at a funeral. As he looked round, Matt also recognized that the staff, except for one secretary and the receptionist, were entirely male. He started to feel quite depressed.

As the interview unfolded it became clear that the company would expect Matt to bring in a number of new clients, and although it wasn't explicitly said, it was implied that he should do this by approaching his family, friends and the people with whom he used to work.

Matt left an hour later knowing that he could never work for that company. He also started to see his public relations job in a different light. After seeing one of the authors of this book (old schoolfriend), he was asked to think about what was important to him – what were his values? – and to start thinking about what his employers were looking for from him.

Matt admitted that he had been assuming that just being a nice guy would be enough to get on, and that he had not been taking his job as seriously as he might. He talked openly about his values and how closely he felt they aligned with the job he already had. The following day he went to work and asked for an interview with his Line Manager. Matt explained his frustrations to his boss, reassured him that he wanted his future to be with the business and asked what he needed to do to get his career back on track and to be re-enthused. Impressed by Matt's honesty, his Line Manager agreed a development plan that would see Matt getting more involved with larger accounts. It was also one that would be aligned to much closer scrutiny so that Matt could demonstrate his abilities.

Matt did leave the company, 14 months later. He was 'poached' by another public relations company, a mark of his improved reputation.

YOUR NOTES

What do others think of you?

Up to this point the analysis has self-focused, about You looking at You. Now we get to the bit where people tend to feel a little more uncomfortable – getting feedback from others.

We tend to fall into two categories when asked to be self-analytical:

- **Overly self-critical.** How often do you hear people say: 'What do you mean you can't do presentations? I've seen you and you were excellent!' – or words to that effect? We do tend to not recognize skills in ourselves that are all too apparent to others.

- **An inflated opinion of our abilities.** How many people do you know who believe that they are excellent at something when in fact they are not very good at all, or even in some cases just plain dreadful?

Now we need to get some feedback from others to test the picture that we have created for ourselves. Of course the simple solution is to just ask people for feedback (use your networks), but there is a simple rule that should be applied:

Because you need objectivity in testing your self-analysis, you should *not* ask for feedback from anyone who is too close to you or knows you too well.

If they know you too well they will probably not ask you the more difficult, challenging questions. Either because they do not want to upset you or, more likely, because they think they know you well enough to know what you are going to say, so why bother asking? Find someone you know and trust, and explain to them that you need this to be a thorough and confidential test. Try your Personnel Department at work (if one exists!), someone you respect from another department, or even another business.

Reality check

Feedback is tough, both to give and to receive

This is where you need to be big and brave, set an example, go up to someone and say: 'Can you give me some feedback, please? I want it warts and all, don't hold back, be completely honest with me – I'm asking you for it and I won't be upset by what you say.'

Your feelings might get a little bruised, but it's wonderfully good for you in the long run and it ensures you're building your Bridge on stone.

The feedback that we should be looking for will come from both official sources and unofficial sources.

What official data exists about you?

Let's start with official sources. We can get this data from a number of areas:

1 Appraisals

Within most organizations you will go through an annual appraisal or performance evaluation process designed to review your performance over the past year and comment on the challenges you have faced and how you met them. Invariably they are conducted by a senior person and will be used to define where they think you have succeeded, or possibly failed. You should remember that this could be based on limited knowledge so it's very important that you keep an accurate record of your work to be able to demonstrate, with examples, what you have done during the period covered by the appraisal. Appraisals can be good for indicating trends and highlighting areas for development activity in search of your goals – particularly if you can amalgamate the results of several appraisals and view them all at the same time. Use them to identify transferable skills. Don't restrict them to what they do for the company you are working for. The need is to highlight those skills that could be taken elsewhere.

360° feedback

Very popular with companies that can afford to do it, this consists of approaching people you have worked with, people who have worked for you and people you have worked for (peers, subordinates and clients), thus obtaining a complete picture of your performance from all angles. It's usually a managed process that uses forms sent to people you identify. The forms can be ones that demand a ranking of some description, require words as feedback, or a combination of both. The forms are completed and returned and the feedback is then combined to give an overview of what all these people think about you. The advantage of this is that it can highlight gaps in performance, indicate the need for development in particular areas, and is based on feedback from people who *do* have some knowledge of you.

Engagement/project satisfaction reports

Businesses have adopted a very project/contract-based approach to managing work and to measuring performance. In this environment many companies use customer satisfaction forms or ask for client feedback reports to find out whether you have done a good job. This gives direct client feedback on *your brand* and how you performed. You need to review these and what they say. Often they are broad, vague and fail to be direct, so you may need to approach the client direct for something more robust. You might feel awkward doing this but what you need is accurate and focused information. Call them up, talk to them directly and ask what you did well, what you can do better, what you need to focus on, get annoyed at and change in your current level of performance.

Use the feedback not only to get better at your job but also to *be seen to be better*, be seen to be trying to improve, be seen to be managing your own reputation and that of the two businesses you are representing – your employers *and* YOU!

2   Interviews

The best of this type of feedback is often given only when you apply for a position within a company. This can take the form of a short interview, tests and skills analysis and interviews to establish whether you have the traits that the potential employer requires. The positive side of this is that it replicates what will happen when you first step in front of a client, go to any interviews and meet a person for the first time. This feedback can be subjective and can be invaluable. If nothing else, it will give you an indication of the first impression that you make on people.

The training company example

One of the authors applied for a job with a large training company by responding to a job advert in a newspaper. The turnover of personnel in this company was very small because of their extremely rigorous recruitment process. The company were quite rightly very proud of this. Looking to recruit just two new members of staff, this is the process they used:

1   **Paper sift.** Initial sift of all applications and reduction of these to a final 90 who would be interviewed.

2   **Social sift.** The 90 were divided into three groups of 30. Each group was then invited to attend an evening briefing that consisted of meeting some members of staff from the company, listening to three half-hour presentations about the company followed by a buffet supper and a chance to mingle. Applicants were interviewed at the start of the evening, and after their departure (promptly at 9.00 p.m.) the company staff reviewed the applicants one at a time using the individuals' photograph to identify them. This was an opportunity for the employees to say 'Yes, I could see this person working with us' or 'No, I don't see this person fitting in with us'.

3   **Peer interview.** The final five applicants were invited to give a 15-minute presentation to a panel of six employees from the company and to then be interviewed by them.

4   **Managing Director interview.** The final five applicants were interviewed one-to-one by the Managing Director.

Nothing unusual in this you might say, except that the parent company insisted that the final agreement to employ the two selected would only be made *after* they had attended a full day of psychometric testing, and this had been rigorously analyzed to ensure a fit with the company ethos, values and way of working.

This may seem extreme, but it worked.

3 Personality tests

Increasingly in today's environment employers try to be sure that you fit their needs, and sometimes they do this by using tests that ask about aspects of your personality. These result in a snapshot of you. The downside to these is that they often require specialized analysis combined with an interview with an assessor who probes for verification of your test results to get an accurate picture.

As with everything else in this book, we must emphasize the need for honesty. Some people try to respond with answers they think the assessors want to see and not the truth. Why? At the end of the day they could end up miserable in a job they're not suited to.

This type of testing is now quite common in the recruitment process. Some of the most common tests, the ones you are most likely to come across, are outlined below.

Reality check

Many people are very sceptical about psychometric testing and even we admit that some of the tests are of only limited value. *But* we do still believe that they can be useful if approached correctly.

We should say that, in all cases, these are *not* pass or fail tests. They are used to examine traits, characteristics or factors about yourself. They can be used to help you identify who you are and what you are like. They are accurate, within limits, and the true measure is: can you see yourself in the feedback given? If you can, make use of it. If you can't, forget it. It's baggage.

Belbin Type
This test was devised to assess team roles and preferred team style. The test itself consists of seven sections, each presenting a number of different statements to which individuals award a number of points. These are then totalled and help indicate individuals' preferred team role and secondary back-up team roles. The roles defined are Company Worker, Chairperson, Shaper, Plant, Resource Investigator, Resource Monitor, Team Worker and Completer-Finisher. It's often a test used when you are to be part of an integrated team or company with a team culture.

Myers-Briggs Type Indicator
A commonly used test that aims to reveal how different personality types behave and give an insight into the individual's character. It comprises 88 questions and an interview with an approved assessor. The four dimensions investigated are: character, attitude to life, whether you act on emotion or logic, and how you organize your life.

Occupational Personality Questionnaire
An examination of 32 different workplace characteristics – these range through reliability, outspokenness and decisiveness and can take anything from 60 to 248 questions. This is an open process where the candidate should be aware of what the questionnaire is, what it is attempting to do, when the results will be available and when feedback will occur.

Learning Style Questionnaire
The Learning Style Questionnaire helps you to identify your preferred learning style. The questionnaire consists of 80 questions, takes approximately 15 minutes to complete and ranks the individual against four distinctive learning styles: activist, pragmatist, reflector and theorist.

Rapid Personality Questionnaire
This covers five personality traits: action, thinking, relating, feeling

and conforming. It's about what you are likely to do rather than what you can and cannot do. Its replies range from 'not like me at all' to 'very like me'. It is a very quick test lasting about 10–20 minutes (depending on how decisive you are).

Sixteen Personality Factor Questionnaire

This consists of 185 questions that are mapped to give an outline of 16 personality factors. It looks at both inside and outside work and, unlike most other tests, has questions on reasoning ability that have right and wrong answers. The test takes 40 minutes and feedback takes place regarding the 16 factors.

DISC/Thomas Profile Analysis

Four characteristics are examined: Dominance, Influence, Steadiness and Compliance (well DISC had to come from somewhere!). Candidates respond to questions with adjectives that best describe them and those adjectives that worst describe them. The theory is that most of us have a preference for one type of behaviour when in work.

Graphology

Whilst many are sceptical about the interpretation of handwriting as a robust method of evaluating individual personality type, the last decade has seen a great increase in the number of companies asking for covering letters to CVs to be handwritten. This practice is particularly popular with American and French companies, and you should be aware that your handwriting may be used during an assessment or as part of a recruitment process.

What unofficial data can you get?

This demands that you do something for yourself and put yourself on the line, because to get this you need to ask for people's feedback and you need to be prepared to face what some people will say. This is hard and can be very uncomfortable as you need to ask people who may not know you well and may not even necessarily get on with you! However, you need their views as much as, if not more than, those of people whom you trust or who are your friends. The key is to face any *shadow issues* (those things that you don't normally want to talk about because they may be uncomfortable or have emotional implications) that do not surface from normal conversations and appraisals.

This is one of the reasons why 360° appraisals are now finding favour. More often these types of appraisals are conducted anonymously so that any colleague raising a shadow issue is protected. The problem with this is that you can obtain an amalgamation of the truth and it doesn't back up statements with supporting arguments or examples. So don't rely on it at face value: ask people for feedback yourself.

The best method is face to face and in small chunks as opposed to by telephone, e-mail, letter or any other method that keeps you at a distance from the person with whom you are communicating. Face to face means that you have their attention and can see them and their reactions.

EXERCISE

You need to do this every day and at every opportunity: do it after meetings, after interviews, after completing and handing in reports or assignments, during drinks, at the water cooler, in the car and at home: after actions, after projects, after presentations — in fact, after anything! Start now, and start building the feedback into your Here & Now, your picture of You plc.

So, who do you ask? Here are some starter ideas, although you should add to it to build your own list. In the future this list will grow and become your network of contacts.

◆ Your family.

◆ Your boss or supervisor.

◆ Your colleagues.

- Your clients.

- Your audiences.

- Your friends and acquaintances.

The types of questions you need to ask are open and requesting feedback – questions that elicit reflection and opinion on you. Below are some examples to help you get started – and remember that you need to ask them in the context of the area you are trying to get feedback on.

- How do I come across?

- What image do I portray?

- How do I affect you and your response to me?

- What do I need to do to improve that response?

- How do you think I can do that?

- How do you feel about me?

- What is it that makes you feel like that?

- What am I good at? Can I improve these areas?

- What am I bad at? How can I improve these areas?

- If I were to do one thing better, what would that be?

This will help you to recognize what you do well. Even if someone is critical, interpret it as something to build on, something constructive. There are no negatives in this, only opportunities.

Example

Comment: 'You are not very good at doing presentations.'

This is a development opportunity for you to work on your presentation skills: attend a course, ask a colleague for help, read a book on the subject. If you can show that you want to learn how to improve in this area it will demonstrate to this person how keen you are to improve.

Remember all the answers help define your brand, your brand's values and how you are regarded – it's your reputation.

YOUR NOTES

What's going on around you?

In a world where there is so much information, how much of it do you take notice of?

Probably not as much as you think, and you probably don't go out of your way as often as you should to get more. Information is power. This is the knowledge economy: those who have information and are able to put it together to their advantage will be the winners. These will be people who are able to:

◆ link together information to gain added value;

◆ network to obtain work and reputation;

◆ make new connections to bring together people, data and methods for competitive advantage;

◆ be creative by bringing together ideas and people who can deliver an end result on behalf of or for others.

How aware are you of the things that are happening around you, and of the changes happening in the economy, or the industry, company, department or team in which you work and operate? Are there other environmental changes that you should be aware of, perhaps affecting your partner's work or the school your children attend – changes that affect your lifestyle as much as your work?

In today's age you need to be wired in to what is happening, what is being said and where you can best use your skills and expertise. We call this *'prairie-dogging'*.

In the wild the prairie dog roams in packs, yet at all times one member of the pack will be looking around for both threats and opportunities. As a free or corporate agent you need to develop this ability to keep your career running, to alert you to potential trouble and to show you where opportunities exist. The sooner you can see the change coming, the sooner you can position yourself for it. And

it helps to have friends you can look out for and swap tips with and
who can help you in return – your pack.

SAP

When we started running the career development workshops we would trawl the
newspapers for examples of how environmental awareness could benefit the
individual. The best example we came across was during the wide-scale adoption of
SAP.

SAP is an accounting software package that was introduced in the mid-nineties and is
now used by a large number of companies in the United Kingdom. In 1997 we would
find only two or three job adverts per newspaper making reference to the need for
SAP experience or knowledge. These jobs were usually offering six-figure salaries for
people able to implement SAP systems. Within a year the number of adverts referring
to SAP had increased dramatically to between 10 and 12 adverts per newspaper. The
salary levels had dropped, but were still high five-figure sums.

By the turn of the century SAP was so commonplace that it was assumed that
accountants would have knowledge of the software, and salaries dropped to a level
that used to be an industry norm.

Any accountant out there in the mid-nineties with an awareness of software packages
who was looking around for opportunities might have spotted this trend, trained up on
SAP and got one of those jobs advertising a six-figure salary. Being aware of your
environment and being proactive within it can reap tangible rewards.

When using the prairie dog example you should become part of a
pack – a group of free agents looking out for each other, or a group of
corporate agents keeping each other informed of what is happening
in different departments or different parts of the industry. You have
probably got it by now – your network is your prairie dog pack. Use
them. Ask them what is going on.

There is an almost infinite amount of information available to us, if we decide to look for it.

When we work, we can be sucked into the mundane and the everyday routine, caught in the 9 to 5 rut, forever focusing on the next task, the next job. Rarely do we take the time to climb out of the rut and take a look around. We might hear the odd rumour at lunch or over a coffee, but not often do we take the time to check it out and make sure that it's true. *You need to start using your senses.*

Sight

Take a look around. How much information is out there that you can use: the papers, the internet, television news, journals, financial or business reports, business and public libraries, magazines, articles, adverts, etc.? By looking around we can gather a large amount of information that is published both internally and externally to our companies. Think about what is being said and what is happening in the world, your skill area and the companies in which you are interested.

Sound: listening and talking

What can you hear with regard to where you are? What are the stories being told or rumours being spread? What is the word on the grapevine? What is being said? What is not being said? And who by? Listen and you can hear what is happening.

Touch

How many people do you know? People matter! Looking around to gather information is fine, but you need to reach out and touch others to get a better feel for what is happening and share information. There is no other way of doing this than to build up a network of contacts. No, we don't mean going around physically touching people, but you do need to start getting in touch with people and keeping in touch with them. Networking!

It is in all honesty who you know and who you can get to know, aligned with what you can offer, that will maintain your employability. You need to connect with people who can tell you what is happening, what their thoughts are on what is happening and where they think things are going. This is the 'Rolodex' approach to your career: the art of staying in contact and connecting with people.

The mistake that many people make is that they are quite happy to rely on e-mail and text messages, thinking that this means networking. These things can help, but there is no substitute for actually meeting people. You need to start showing up and hanging around. *You need to be seen.*

It's a bit cheeky, but we're replacing smell and taste here with that other sense …

The sixth sense

For all the use of the recognized five senses there is often a strong reliance on another, our sixth sense: intuition. Often even when you have gathered all the information you can, your gut feeling tells you something different.

Paul's story

The company was doing well and Paul had what he thought was a secure and reliable job. But when he started looking around, a different picture began to emerge.

Externally, the industry was retrenching, companies were merging, the market was slack and overpopulated and it was apparent that a large number of companies were all vying for a limited amount of business.

Paul, whilst aware of what was happening outside, was still receiving the official internal 'business is great' message and accepted it as true. He noticed that his manager was more distant and that, increasingly, a number of senior managers were off-site. His intuition told him that something was wrong, but he still chose to accept the company line.

Three weeks later Paul was made redundant.

You need to be scanning all your sources for their richness and diversity to enable you to have a constant health check of what is happening. If we examine this process, the following model will help you build up a picture.

Reality check

If you think that intuition is exaggerated, think about job interviews. Most interviewers will make a decision about an individual's suitability within a minute of them entering the room based on their gut feeling as to whether someone would fit in and whether they look the part.

So where can you get environmental information from?

By using your senses properly you can access so much information from a large range of sources. Here are some suggestions to get you started:

◆ **Media.** Papers, journals, magazines, internet postings, internet interest groups, job adverts, company reports and press releases, internal publications, other career books, contract and order notices.

◆ **Network.** People you work with, the water cooler conversationalists, the smokers' corner / room, your friends, external associates, customers, suppliers, recruitment agencies and recruitment consultants, former colleagues and bosses, former acquaintances, training colleagues, professional associations.

> **EXERCISE**
>
> Take 20 minutes and list all your current sources of information.
> Take another 10 and work out what gaps exist! The more you know,
> the better you can weather any storm.

Use the following questions and fill in the gaps for your situation.

Information sources:

◆ Who knows the most about my field?

◆ Who do I know who can put me in touch with that person?

◆ Who has information I can use to build my skills at home or at work?

◆ Who can provide guidance in solving problems, or help me figure out what my next action should be?

◆ If I don't know that person, do I know someone who does?

Think. The more you know, the more power you have.

Support groups:

◆ Who are the people around me who are 'in the same boat'?

◆ Have I done any favours for friends? Who are they?

◆ Which of my friends do I enjoy exchanging ideas and experiences with?

◆ Which of my friends and colleagues recognize and appreciate my skills and accomplishments?

These are people you can use as sounding boards. For instance, why not 'try out' that new idea before presenting it to top management? No need to give away all the details. Present it as a concept to a few people in your network and check the response.

Family, friends, acquaintances:

♦ Who do I know (don't forget distant relatives) who works in the same or related field as I do?

♦ Who, of all the people I know, is the best networker? (Get these people to help you network – they'll love it!)

♦ Have I let everyone know I'm looking for a job? Did I tell my: friends, family, doctor, solicitor, dentist, accountant, neighbours, former employers, colleagues, club members, sports team members?

Future possibilities:

♦ Who are the people I'd most like to meet (someone I heard speak at a conference, someone a friend or colleague spoke highly of, etc.)?

♦ How can I get in touch with those people?

♦ Are there any clubs, organizations or associations I can join that will put me in contact with the kinds of people I want to meet?

♦ Do I know anyone, or is there anyone I want to know, who can make me think, who will challenge me to grow?

♦ How can I find these people? (Networking is very much like solving a puzzle: finding one clue leads you to the next and the next. One contact refers you to another, who refers you to another, until you find that one contact who will provide you with the solution you need.)

♦ How can I do my own 'public relations'? Is there a newsletter, local newspaper, trade magazine or journal I can tell about my promotion, successful presentation, etc.?

Think of an example

Almost everyone we know got the jobs they are in now because of the networks that they have utilized. In those few exceptions when people have got jobs by responding to job adverts, their careers have then progressed because of the networks they have built.

Think about the people you know and see how many examples you can think of of people who either got jobs, or have progressed in their jobs/careers by networking effectively. How did they do it? How can you do it?

Christine's story

Christine is employed by a very large public sector company. When she started working for the company she was recruited to fill a lower middle management role. Being ambitious, Christine twice applied for promotion, but on both occasions she failed at interview to demonstrate the skills necessary for the higher position.

Getting increasingly frustrated, Christine persuaded a friend who worked in another department to find her a job there, in an area where she was not known. She moved across and, aware of her own limitations, decided the best way forward was to socialize and network like crazy. Initial progress was slow, but then Christine found herself presented with an opportunity that would be too good to miss.

Christine applied for a team management role that no one else wanted, and got it. This meant a significant promotion (to a senior management grade) and a great deal of extra responsibility. Christine knew that she did not have the skills for the job, so she identified two friends who had the skills needed to help her and brought them into her team. She then divided her responsibilities equally between the two whilst she continued to socialize and network.

When another opportunity presented itself, Christine applied for and got another promotion, but only on the understanding that her two colleagues would move with her.

At the time of writing this book Christine is applying for another promotion and is, on the face of things, doing extremely well. Her success, by her own admission, has been based on her ability to network.

Unfortunately, this is a cautionary tale. Whilst networking is important, you must still ensure that you have the skills needed for any role that you take. In Christine's case she has relied almost entirely on two people to do her job for her. One of these people, recognizing what was happening, has now left the business. The one remaining colleague has recently married and is planning on giving up work soon to start a family. Christine's time is limited. She has to find someone else to do her job for her or face the fact that she is going to be found out.

A large number of people are watching her progress with interest at the moment!

YOUR NOTES

What does You plc look like now?

After reading this chapter, you should have looked thoroughly at:

◆ your skill set;

◆ your values, linking them to career anchors;

◆ getting feedback, official and unofficial;

◆ environmental awareness, prairie-dogging and networking.

You should now have started to build up a picture of You plc. This picture lists who you are, what you can do, what your values are, how they align to your company's values, what others think of you, who is in your network, how you access environmental information and what is going on around you.

So what sort of picture is it? Does it paint a future so bright you have to wear shades, or are you the captain of a sinking ship?

Take heart! We know that the picture is rarely that rosy at first. Why else would you be reading this book! The goal is to learn from what you now have and plan where you want to go.

'The farther backward you can look, the further forward you are likely to see.'

Winston Churchill

The advantage you now have is that you have reflected on what has brought you to this point. You have identified your strengths and you should be proud of them. You have also learned that there are some areas of You plc that need work – and that is a good thing!

This is who you are now, your starting point, your Here & Now. If you don't want to, you don't have to stay here – if you don't like it, you can change it.

- Maybe we can see where we need more information and a better network.

- Maybe we can recognize what we can offer the market *now* and what reward and recognition that may bring.

- Maybe we now have a better understanding of our skills, abilities and competencies and how we can extend them, use them and bring them to the career marketplace. Some of these may be attributes that we had not realized that we had before.

- Maybe we can see gaps that need filling.

But this is not the end, it is just the starting line. We have defined one riverbank, the Here & Now. From here we need to start looking at how You plc can identify the other riverbank, the There & Then. Once we have done that, we can look at how we build the Bridge from one to the other.

Ready? Let's go and look at the future!

05

chapter five
there & then

Okay. By now you should have built a robust and honest picture of who you are, right here and now. This is your snapshot that will be your starting point for planning your career. What you have just completed gives you the basic building blocks that you can use to determine:

◆ what you want;

◆ what you need;

◆ where you want to go;

◆ when you want to get there.

In other words, it can start helping you to define not only your career aspirations and goals but also your lifestyle requirements *and* help you to understand what is achievable and realistic. Be aware of what we've already discussed about becoming more aware of your changing work environment and your personal brand. Remember that *change is constant and inevitable*!

Within the ever-moving boundaries that define these fast-moving times, you are now in a position to start taking ownership of and responsibility for your career direction. This chapter explains what you need to consider in order to work out where you want to be (the There & Then) and will help you decide what you want your future to look like.

Reality check

At this point you may be thinking: *'Here we go, they're going to give us lots of stuff about "living the dream" and "be the best that you can be".* *I've heard it all before.'* Yes, of course we want you to 'live the dream' and 'be the best that you can be'. If we didn't we wouldn't have written this book! But hopefully our approach is a little different from the other self-help books out there.

We believe that you *can* view your future in a different light and, with the belief that you have what it takes to make a significant change for the better, that you *can* take ownership and responsibility and that the answers *do* lie hidden within you. We think that you get to those answers not by entering into some sort of trance to enter your deep psyche but by looking at what we've done so far and applying a sensible, common-sense process to deciding which elements of it you really *want* to keep in your future. That's it.

Let's start by explaining what we mean by 'There & Then'.

- ◆ **There.** Where do we want to get to? If you were to imagine what you want your life, your job and your environment to look like in the future, how would it look? (Now try again without the lottery win and be a bit more realistic this time!)

- ◆ **Then.** When would you like to achieve this by? (Again, be realistic.)

The important thing here is that you need to start with the *Big Picture*.

One of the big things that we've learned in the last few years of doing this is that there are a few things that you need to consider before we get truly stuck into There & Then. So, before we get too excited, let's spend a few minutes raising your awareness of some of the wider issues that we need to consider.

What do you want?

Your answer to this question might help you determine your answers to later exercises. What do you want from life? Is it money, time, freedom, adventure, power or something else entirely? Different people will have picked up this book for all sorts of different reasons. For example:

◆ to take control of their lives;

◆ to improve their current position, but they are not sure how;

◆ to gain an understanding of what they can do about their future;

◆ to learn how to get promotion or to change role;

◆ curiosity.

What do you want?

Let's be more specific:

◆ **Family.** Do you have family who are important to you and must be considered as part of any plan? What would they think of any change you want to make? Does it affect them? Can they help you make this change? Do you require their permission?

◆ **Location.** Will any changes require you to move? What will that mean in the context of your family and friends? Do you have the finances to move to where you need to relocate to? Will your lifestyle remain the same when you have moved? How will a move affect your children's schooling, partner's work and relationships with friends and family?

◆ **Lifestyle.** What changes will occur in your lifestyle? Will it change your income level? Will you lose contact with friends and family? What will you have to give up to make this happen? Can you do without your Saturday nights out and the Hugo Boss jeans? How will it affect your involvement with the sports club, the amateur dramatic society or any other social activity / group?

- **Current career.** Will you be able to maintain your current level of performance in your current position? Will additional training be required? Can you get through this training within your current career or will you need to work during evenings or at weekends?

- **Income.** Do you have enough to support you during a change? If not, what additional financial help is required and where can you get it?

- **Values.** By moving for more money, will you impact upon your values? By moving to feel valued, will you accept a drop in value (i.e. less money)? If you make a change to where you feel you add greater value, will you still be as valued?

Ryan's story

When Ryan looked at his lifestyle it became apparent that something was missing. A family man, he and his family had moved because of his job to a new area some seven years ago. They had made friends, but, as with many career-orientated people, Ryan had obtained further promotion, which often took him away from the area in which they were now living and his family were becoming increasingly isolated from their family and past friends. His wife was increasingly on her own dealing with the home and family and she was beginning to feel more and more detached, isolated and dissatisfied.

In assessing their lifestyle the following facts were obvious:

- The job would continue to take Ryan away from home on a regular basis.

- The current home was reasonable, but not really located well for a growing family.

- The increasing sense of isolation was putting a strain on all parties.

Once these things had been discussed, Ryan and his wife made the decision to relocate back to where they had previously lived. Ryan accepted that this would involve more travelling and nights away from home for him, but the family would be near relatives and friends and in an area more suited to their needs.

This was a lifestyle choice that suited the whole family and not just Ryan as an individual. Of course, this choice had a price (that Ryan would be away from home more often), but it was a price that Ryan and his family considered acceptable.

While this example doesn't show the full range of questioning that lifestyle assessment needs, it does show that choices have to be made at each and every level and this is even more true for the free agent. Before you set out on any journey you need to consider what the impact will be on other areas of your life – that's why we always refer to *reality checks*. There is *always* a price. Without a reality check it is difficult to know what the price will be or whether you're willing to pay it. It would be great to think that you, or we, could decide to give up what we are doing now and start doing something else without a care in the world. However, for one of us here, Gary, his wife would certainly have something to say about that!

What do you want your future to look like?

When you start defining where you want to be, you need to consider that this is not just about a job or a role within an organization. It might not even be about having just one job – in a free agent world you can have as many jobs as you want. What this is about is ensuring that you have a balanced lifestyle. All those areas that we asked you about before should be considered within the whole: family, location, lifestyle (including your social life), current career, income and values. There may be other considerations such as spirituality, health or education.

You also need to be thinking radically differently about time-scales. To make changes like these it would be a waste of time taking a short-term view. You need to start thinking long-term.

Long-term success is often born out of long-term strategies. Isn't that what you want for yourself? To do this properly will involve adopting a surprisingly different mind-set. The culture we are used to expects us to deliver results within six or twelve months or within the current financial year – oh, and let's make that a bonus target for you. But here you're trying to make a significant change in your life – you need to take your time and do it right.

With something as long-term as career planning it's vital that we start by defining a major long-term goal (anything from two to twenty years) from which we can then work out a whole series of short-term targets, each one up to six or twelve months in duration.

The reason for this is that people overestimate what can be achieved in a year (e.g. gaining a professional qualification) and vastly underestimate what can be achieved in five years. It's also true that some goals take time that can't be short-cut. You need to set your long-term goals to know what the other side of the Bridge, the There & Then, is going to look like. You always need to know where you are going and what you are working towards. On the days when things get tough or don't go according to plan, we all need a little reminder of why we are doing things. Having that long-term target will always give you something to focus on.

At this stage most of you won't have a clear idea of what your long-term goal is, so this chapter is about identifying your desired future state or position, your desired set of elements within your life and a list of priorities. Only then can we start to identify what we need to do to get there.

Peter's story

Peter attended one of the workshops that we ran. He was a quiet man in his mid-forties, married with two children and team leader of a small group of specialists. Peter said he was at the workshop because, as a specialist in charge of a team of specialists, he had effectively reached a career ceiling in his field. He didn't know where his career could take him next. But when we talked to him in more detail we discovered that his major concern was not his career prospects or building a career plan for the future, it was about reorganizing his whole life.

Peter's wife was much younger than him and had dedicated the last few years to having their children and bringing them up. She had also used this time to study for and pass an Open University degree and now, with the children both at school, Peter was conscious that her career was about to start. Because she was not restricted by specialization in the same way, he realized that her career prospects and earning potential exceeded his own. He also felt that his age was a factor in that by the time he re-skilled he would be around 50 and thought he would subsequently be less attractive to potential employers. Peter was having to consider his own career in terms of his family's priorities.

By the end of the workshop Peter was talking about how he felt that he needed to support his wife in the same way that she had supported him during the years that their children had been growing up. He felt that he was now prepared to slow down his own career development, perhaps even taking a 'backward' step to a role with less responsibility. This would enable him to spend more time looking after his children, giving his wife time to pursue a career of her own.

Everyone is in a different situation and everyone has different priorities, but the same rules apply in any of the areas that we have asked you to consider. Think about income, for example. What is the minimum level of income that you and your dependants can survive on – how much do you need for your mortgage, bills, holidays, etc., day to day? If you choose a career option that will not pay you enough for this, what are you going to give up? Or does that career option get put into the 'unrealistic' bin straight away? You need to start considering your desired future state by giving consideration to all aspects of your life.

Reality check: an aside

Reflecting on Peter's story, it has occurred to us that there is something else we should mention – age. Many of the delegates who have attended our workshops have been approaching retirement or thinking of taking early retirement. In almost every case they arrived with the attitude that they should only be thinking about their remaining years with the business, but this is ridiculous.

Life expectancy in the UK in 2001 was 80 for men and slightly more for women. If you retire at 50, 55 or 60, what are you going to do with the remaining 20+ years of your life? Golf? Gardening? House cleaning? An increasing number of 'retired' people are using their considerable experience to go and do something they have always wanted to do.

Peter's concerns about his age are becoming increasingly outdated. In your planning you must not limit yourself to thinking about a retirement age. You have more time than you think!

Values

In any future planning you also need to consider what your values are and whether they align with the businesses and people you are planning to work with. Increasingly in the fast pace of today, as we choose the type of lifestyle we want, we find that our values and those of others/employers clash. This creates stress for the individual and in the relationship between the individual and the organization in which they work and often that stress is released away from work on unsuspecting family and friends, or by being self-destructive. Values are as important as any of the lifestyle components; they're not just something related to work.

Values and the free agent

The free agent can work outside this trap by trading the supposed 'loyalty' contract with a business for the 'freedom' of independence. By working as a free agent or independent consultant, the match between individual values and those of the environment in which that individual works can be better managed and maintained because they choose. The trade in this case is that the individual is accepting more risk and insecurity in exchange for the life they want to lead. This can result in different stresses, so if you choose this route, you need to be aware of them and be able to manage them – it's the price you pay. As a free agent, the best environment will be one in which the company's values and yours match. Not only will this make it a more pleasant environment in which to work, but it will quickly give you a sense of belonging.

But what about people who either can't make that choice or choose to accept whatever values and restrictions a business imposes on them?

Values and the corporate agent

For most of us who want to manage our career and make our own choices, there is often a third party involved: our employer. Many of us are not lucky enough to be living in a free agent world, or we have decided that we don't want that level of risk in our lives. Instead, we live in a corporate world – a world ruled by others' values, regulations and bureaucracy.

We are the corporate slaves: people used to burying our own values, aspirations, needs and beliefs for a pay cheque at the end of the month.

In many companies the stated values are a reflection of what the senior managers think they should be saying as opposed to being what they truly believe or live. If you understand that, you have a better chance of living with them and accepting your lot. You still need to be aware of the company's values, be aware of your own, and aware of the match or mismatch between the two so that when you move on from your current position, department or company you can ensure a better fit.

As you start becoming more aware of your corporate environment, what you see around you can often be frustrating. Inefficiency, people who don't care and people who complain and whinge but do nothing for themselves. Our advice … Forget them, leave them with their own problems! Don't try to help them because often they don't want help. The only way they'll take ownership of themselves and take responsibility for their career and make a change is if they decide to get off their own backsides. Instead, concentrate on yourself and how you can use the system to meet both your needs and the needs of the business. Focus on the win-win – a win for you and a win for them. You can do this and keep moving to a new future – think 'line of sight'.

Line of sight

The majority of businesses today demand that any development activity, training intervention or business improvement action must be aligned to that business's goals and vision, so much so that managers and executives often sign off that activity with 'line of sight' in evidence (see Figure 5.1).

'Line of sight' is a consultancy term that implies that for any action or step taken, you must be able to see its impact against a nominated

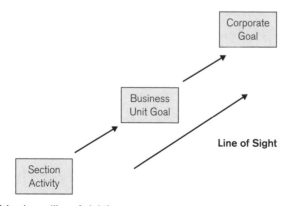

Figure 5.1 *A business 'line of sight'*

strategic goal. In other words, it must have a positive benefit on the company and where the company wants to be.

The story of the Consultancy Services

The Consultancy Services (CS) is an internal management consultancy working as part of a large public sector industry within the United Kingdom.

In the mid-nineties everyone working in management wanted to have an MBA (Masters in Business Administration) – it was the management fad of the age – and the employees of CS were no exception. For a couple of years the company agreed almost all requests for MBAs, until they suddenly realized how much it was costing. Without controls in place, employees could attend courses and get qualifications that bore no resemblance to the core skills of the business or its strategic goals. As part of a public sector industry, CS was also conscious of the need to be seen to be effectively managing its expenditure. As the number of requests for MBAs grew, CS decided that some controls needed to be put in place.

They introduced the CS Scholarship Application Form and anyone applying for funding for a professional qualification had to submit one of these forms. In one question on the form the applicant was asked to explain how this particular qualification fitted with the strategic needs of the business. The form had to be endorsed by a sponsor (i.e. Line Manager, board member, etc.) before submission.

As a result, the number of requests for professional qualifications, including MBAs, dropped by 75%, but those that were submitted were almost entirely agreed because they could clearly demonstrate 'line of sight'.

As individuals, it's important that we use the same method. (Remember, You plc is a business – so run it like one!) That is, create a 'line of sight' that positively impacts on where you want to go. Any action or activity we take must be judged in line with where we want to get to and by when (Figure 5.2).

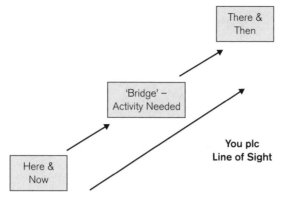

Figure 5.2 *You plc 'line of sight'*

If you work in a given business or corporation, you are probably expected to demonstrate line of sight with any activity you undertake. What we are suggesting is that, whilst being careful to fulfil the goals of the corporation, you should also be considering how that same activity fits with your personal line of sight. Do it properly and you can get the two lines of sight to overlay quite nicely, but you can only do this if you are aware of the overlap in the first place.

Wouldn't it be nice to be in a business or a role where the two lines of sight are exactly the same, where you and the business want exactly the same things? Unfortunately, corporations often forget this need.

'Some of the dullest days I have spent in my 18 years as a wage-slave have been on training courses. Training is good only if it succeeds in teaching you something useful. But most of it doesn't, or doesn't do it effectively'.

Lucy Kellaway, *Sense and Nonsense in the Office*

When you see a corporate goal, start trying to identify what's in it for you. Ask yourself: how can I achieve what is required by the company and move myself towards my goal at the same time? Alternatively: what do I need to achieve my goal, and how closely can I align that with a need of the business? The aim is to look for the

Figure 5.3 *Corporate goals and your goals overlap*

overlap of the two and use it to guide your choices (Figure 5.3). Do it right and maybe you could find that the business is supporting and funding the development you need for your personal line of sight.

Unless there's some 'What's In It For Me?' element in anything you do, then why are you doing it? Unless there is something that you can gain from completing a piece of work or an activity, you'll be bored, demotivated and lethargic. Try to concentrate your efforts on doing the things that you want to do and the things you absolutely *have* to do.

The end and the beginning

Okay – that's the end of the areas that we felt that we had to introduce to you and to get you to take into consideration when looking for There & Then. In conclusion:

◆ **Balance your lifestyle.** Consider the impact on all aspects of your life when making a career change.

◆ **Time-scales.** This is important, so don't rush it!

◆ **Values.** Understand your own from Here & Now and those of the business and people that affect you.

◆ **Line of sight.** Every activity should take You plc closer to your personal goals.

This is the beginning of starting you to think about There & Then, before the next chapter, in which we offer you some tools to help you on your way.

Where do you want to go?

Often the hardest part of being where you are is deciding where you want to go. How many of us take the time to really consider what we want to be doing? We go to work, come home from work, but we don't often switch off. Be honest – have you ever worked at a weekend? And it's not just work that is fast-paced – often we get home stressed from the pace of work and find ourselves managing a home, a family, a social life, etc., that are all equally fast-paced, often as stressful, and always as time-consuming. A two-week holiday is often the only way to get some downtime, and it's often only then that you are relaxed enough to begin to think about where you are and what has been going on around you. And the free agent often has it no better, worrying about where the next contract is coming from and what the next change in work will bring. To work out where you want to go you *must* make time to dream! If you don't think about the future, then you're in danger of being left behind and you will have to work twice as hard to catch up.

'Standing still is the fastest way of moving backwards in a rapidly changing world.'

Said by someone important, but no one seems to know who

You hear about people who have jobs that pay fantastically well, but who are unfulfilled and unhappy. Take time to think about what you really want.

Gone are the days when good things were handed to you because you stood out from the masses. Nowadays you are likely to be expected to manage your own progress, particularly in more senior jobs. These statements are taken from a recruitment pack of a well-known blue chip company:

◆ To understand your current position and recognize the gaps you have when considering the complete role.

◆ To research and investigate methods to close the gaps found during job analysis.

◆ To identify the next role and the potential for career advancement whilst considering the need for succession management within the business.

It's time for you to decide what you want to do with your career.

Adam's story

Adam had been working for eight years as a Project Manager in a large logistics company. He found the work interesting, comfortable and safe, but neither challenging nor difficult.

Adam's colleagues started to realize that he was working longer and longer hours and many thought that he'd either taken on more work, or was trying to position himself for promotion. But despite the long hours appearing on his timesheets, Adam was in fact doing no more work than before. Eventually his Line Manager intervened, sat Adam down, and tried to find out what was going on. It transpired that Adam and his wife were having difficulties in their relationship and that his home life had become so stressful that Adam had been spending more and more time in the office – his comfortable, safe haven. Adam agreed to take some time off to spend with his wife to try to resolve their issues.

Whilst addressing the issues in his relationship, Adam found himself doing some very serious self-analysis for the first time in his life. He realized that he'd accepted the comfortable career because he thought that was expected of him and not because it was what he wanted. In re-assessing his priorities, Adam recognized the importance of his marriage and that he wanted to spend more time working on that part of his life. He also recognized the need to be doing something positive and motivational with his life. He was frustrated by not being able to work in areas that were more interesting and challenging to him, specifically Interior Design, and he started to explore how he could move into these new areas.

For Adam the key was that whilst he had an interest in Interior Design founded on all the DIY he'd done at home, he had no formal training or background. With the support of his wife, Adam came up with a plan.

◆ He enrolled at night school to study some aspects of Interior Design to confirm his interest in this as an option.

◆ He returned to work, but renegotiated his contract, taking a cut in salary, to work four days a week.

be your own career consultant

momentum

◆ He then wrote to various Interior Design magazines and offered to work for them, free of charge, for one day a week so that he could find out more about the industry.

Eighteen months later Adam had successfully completed four separate night school courses. He had enrolled to study Interior Design at a college in London on an open learning course and had a CV that included 18 months' experience of working in the industry. With the full support of his wife Adam resigned from his comfortable and safe job and went to work in Interior Design for a start-up company launching a new magazine.

Adam loves his job and he loves his life. He has re-assessed his priorities, he is working in a field that he loves, he is enjoying the 'risk' and the new challenges. His only regret is that he didn't decide to make the change sooner.

Perfection

The lifestyle that you want does not necessarily exist in one job or role. When you think about what you really want to do and break it down into its component elements, you may find that some of those things you consider very important do not involve work at all and that you have to look elsewhere for them. Similarly, you may find that you cannot identify one job that gives you everything you want, and that maybe for you the optimal career path is to have more than one job, or to work in a job that allows you the time and space to pursue other interests. When you define your personal *There*, including your lifestyle requirements, you must be open-minded enough to know that you will not necessarily find it in one place. Of course this plays very much into the hands of the free agent. We feel that you can be a free agent wherever you are, so look around. The independent free agent has the flexibility to work in several different fields at the same time – but so does the free agent employed by a company. Accept that perfection may mean getting 8 out of 10 if the other 2 out of 10 can be achieved in another part of your life (see 'Elements' Chapter 6).

Motivation

Stuart has an old copy of *What Color is Your Parachute?* by Richard
Nelson Bolles and in the front of this book is a cartoon from the
Charlie Brown collection in which one of the characters, Linus, says
to Snoopy (the dog hero of the cartoons):

'Here's something to think about. Life is like a ten-speed bicycle
… Most of us have gears that we never use!'

Linus is absolutely correct – it *is* something to think about.

You got your current job because you had several skills that were
needed to fill that role. We are willing to bet that if you look back at
Chapter 3 you will see that you have many other skills that you
could be using on a daily basis. The more of these skills you are
encouraged to use, the more appreciated you feel, the more fulfilled
you feel and, therefore, the more motivated you are! Simple.

A tip

If you see a job advertised, before you decide to apply, compare your Here
& Now (You plc) with the job description. Ask yourself a couple of
questions: 'Does You plc look like the person they are describing in the
advert? How many gears would you be using in this job and, therefore, how
motivated will you be?'

See how many jobs you suddenly realize you were only attracted to
because of the job title, the salary or the location, and how many of these
would really be unfulfilling and demotivating.

When do you want to get there?

Only after you have identified the *There* you want to achieve can you
start to think about when you want to get there (the *Then*). How long
are you willing to take before you reach your goal? For some of you,

you will want it now! For others, it will be a something that has a series of steps that results in reaching the goal after a given period of time.

You need to ask:

◆ What development is necessary? (What is the skill gap?)

◆ How can I best achieve that development? (What is best for me – a course, book learning, on-the-job training?)

◆ How long will it take me? (If there are several gaps, can I do them concurrently or do I have to do them one after the other?)

Only then can you work out, realistically, what is achievable in terms of time-scales.

As a free agent, the planning horizon will be short because in the marketplace you will need to consider periods of re-skilling to ensure that you remain employable. On the other hand, if you are working within a company, you can look at planning as a more long-term affair and take more time over it. The other possible advantage is that, if the line of sights of You plc and the employer are aligned, the company may be paying the bill.

So what should you be considering?

Planning horizons years 2–20

Long-term planning takes into account the needs of where you want to go on a large scale. This is strategy stuff involving changes that need to be broken down to a finite number of steps, each helping with the accumulation of additional skills. At this stage you need to think carefully about your *priorities*. Which is more important, your job satisfaction, or maintaining an earning level that will see your youngest child through their final two years at school? Lifestyle stuff. Change Loop stuff.

Planning year 1

With short- to medium-term planning we are generally talking about the current year. These are the activities distilled down from your long-term plan and can be considered stepping stones to take you to your ultimate goal (the Bridge to your There & Then).

As in business planning, you need to have definite, achievable steps mapped out. You need to have them time-tabled in, telling you what needs to be done, by when, and how the changes will be made and managed. The principles to use are the same as those given above, but limited to the shorter time-scale.

In some cases the one-year planning steps can get down to as simple as a phone call to a university or research over the internet. At other times it is the need to attend a training course or read a particular book. The key is always to remember your goal and the 'line of sight', then create actions that always take you a step closer to the goal and not a step further away.

Reality check

Time and pace are very, very difficult to manage and we are conscious that one of the messages here may be ambiguous. We keep emphasizing how fast-moving the pace of change is, and yet we are saying don't rush, take your time and do it properly. Yes, both statements are correct!

If the There & Then that you wish to aim at is a major change in your life then you *must*, for your own good, ensure that you do it robustly. Only by being thorough will you ensure that the change is managed effectively and that it will be 'sticky' once it is achieved and won't fall apart six months later.

Whilst going through this possibly slow and drawn-out process, you *must* be constantly vigilant about the changes in the environment which may impact upon your There & Then, and be ready to react to them or incorporate them as necessary.

One of the reasons why we place a lot of faith in the Elements tool (in the next chapter) is that it allows us to be flexible and reactive. You need to be the same.

To market or not to market?

You are in charge of your career within the company and you have to manage your own reputation, not only with customers and with the bosses, but with everyone within your environment. *Never* underestimate the importance of your peers, your boss's secretary, the receptionist or the cleaner. They can all influence your reputation and your future. You therefore need to decide how you should market You plc to best position yourself towards your There & Then. To put it another way: if a business spends a lot of time and money marketing itself, how are you going to market You plc?

However, it's no good defining your own brand unless you are prepared to *live it every day*. Your brand is only defined through self-analysis (see Chapter 3) and you need to understand that for everything you do you must ask: 'Does this support and enhance my brand, or does it diminish it? Does it improve my reputation? Am I happy and comfortable with it? Does it reflect what I want other people to think of me?'

You will need to apply your brand to everything you do. Make managing your personal reputation a major consideration in every decision that you take. Start shaping your life now, using what you discovered in Chapter 3 to start shaping yourself and other people's opinions of you. We'll develop your personal brand in more detail in the next chapter.

Reality check

It's easy for us to say all of this to you, but it is difficult to apply and will take effort on your part. It will also take some subtlety, sensitivity and flexibility. Some people may notice the change and may react badly to it – you should be prepared to hide it if required. And sometimes you will see someone else's brand working and you should take time out to study it and adapt elements of it into your own brand to achieve your needs. You should always be examining and adapting your brand, but it should be consistent; and once you have defined your brand and are happy with it, then you must live it – *all the time.*

In summary …

It seems that we've thrown a great deal at you here, but that's good! There is an enormous amount that you need to consider when trying to decide on your There & Then, and if you are realizing that, then we've done our job. All of the messages we have covered here are important, but the key ones are:

◆ There & Then is not necessarily about one job or role.

◆ You must consider all the elements of your life to give you balance in order to realize your potential.

◆ The free agent mentality is not just about people acting independently; it can be applied in the corporate world.

◆ When considering the Then by which you want to achieve your goals, don't try to rush: be realistic and be patient.

◆ Use Chapter 3 to help you define the brand for You plc.

chapter six
tools – think harder

be your own career consultant

momentum

There & Then tools: dreaming with structure

In this chapter we'll introduce you to the tools to help you think about where You plc wants to be in the future, whether that's in twelve months' time, in five years or even ten years from now. As with the Here & Now tools, take the time to complete each exercise and reflect on the answers you give. Together these will help you to define what you want your future to look like, and the clearer the picture, the easier it will be to identify the route you should take.

The underlying question here is, what do you want to change about Here & Now? In this chapter we will introduce you to six tools:

◆ Futurology.

◆ Element analysis.

◆ Vision.

◆ Direction, speed planning and career actions.

◆ Goal setting.

◆ Brand management.

Whilst each of these tools can be used in isolation to help with specific areas, *we strongly encourage you to use them all collectively* to give you the most robust assessment possible. Unlike the Here & Now tools, these tools will take more thought, consideration and imagination, and consequently may take you longer to get results that make you happy. Don't worry, this is common, but we would encourage you again to use the *'Your Notes'* pages at the end of each tool (or whatever other method suits you best) to write down your thoughts. Carry the notes with you so that you can add to them when thoughts occur to you. As before, you need to be completely honest with yourself if you want to get results that will make you happy.

> **Reality check**
> One problem you will face is that some of the changes that you try to introduce will be intangible – changes inside you, perhaps to your attitudes or values. This is difficult because it makes it hard to measure the change. To quote the late Douglas Adams – *'Don't Panic!'* (*The Hitchhiker's Guide to the Galaxy*). If the changes have been effective, *you will know* – you will feel it.

What do you want to change exactly?

In the previous chapter we emphasized the need to make time away from all external influences (and particularly our jobs) to consider what we want from our lives. You are going to need to do that now. Not necessarily all at once, but perhaps for a couple of hours a day, you *must* make time to think about and plan your next steps.

It is no use setting out to change the Here & Now if you are limited by something that you are unwilling to, or cannot negotiate to, change. In the previous chapter we asked you to consider a number of questions about your lifestyle and what you want against a series of headings: family, location, lifestyle, current career, income and values. You now need to start by reviewing some of those areas and considering what you would like to change, what the cost would be, and also what you don't want to change.

As you answer the questions we pose, write down your answers and how you came to them – they are important!

Let's start by looking at futurology and expanding the list we asked you to consider in 'what do you want?'.

Futurology

1 Location.

2 Way of working.

3 Family.

4 Resources.

5 Skills.

6 Finances.

7 Values.

8 Belief.

1 Location

◆ Think about where you live. Is it a place where you want to stay? Do you want to leave? Do you enjoy living in the city, or do you just enjoy visiting for the day? Are you limited by location? Are you willing to move? Where would you be willing to move to?

People feel at home in different places. For some it is the buzz of a big city, New York or London, whilst for others the city is, at best, somewhere that they like to visit occasionally, and, at worst, a nightmare of noise and dirt. Which do you prefer? Or do you want the best of both worlds: to work in the city all week and travel home to peace and quiet at the weekend? When you have considered the There & Then for You plc, you will need to have given this consideration. Can your There & Then be achieved in your current location, and, if not, what are you going to do about it?

David's story

David was working as a Systems Analyst for a large corporation until he found himself under threat of redundancy. At the time he was living in a nice area, was married and had three children, all at school.

Using his contacts, David was able to find two vacancies in other companies that would have suited him extremely well. There was little difference between the two positions except in two areas: salary and location. In one vacancy the salary offered was considerably higher, but it would have meant relocating to an area north of London, a considerable distance from their current location.

David discussed the options with his wife and she was happy to support him in whatever decision he made. The crucial factor in the end was that David's middle child was taking his GCSEs that year. David took the local vacancy with the lower salary because he believed that the change of location would have been detrimental to his son's education.

2   Way of working

◆ How do you like to work? What suits you best? Does where you are now offer the opportunities that you require? What sort of company do you want to work for? Do you want to work for yourself? Will your values restrict you? What are the things that you will not give up? What are the things you must avoid? Which of these things would you compromise on, if any?

You need to decide what it is that you want as a way of working. Answer these questions and jot down why you have made these choices.

◆ Fixed hours or flexible hours?

◆ Office-based or home-based?

◆ Work alone or as part of a team?

- Told what to do or telling what to do?

- Suit or casual?

- Bureaucratic or trusting? (Bureaucracy does not necessarily mean lack of trust, but do you want to be constantly filling in time-sheets showing what you have been doing with every last ten minutes of your day?)

- Travel or one location?

- Lots of clients or just one client?

- Fixed income or irregular income?

- Shift work or not?

Consider which of the following situations you'd like to be in. Again, consider why you have made the choice you have.

- A free agent – working independently, your own boss, working hard to maintain your reputation and your network, but able (to a degree) to pick and choose the work that you do, often at good recharge rates.

- A corporate worker – tied to a role but with the security of contract and all the issues that go with corporate life. However, this may give you the time to develop your interests outside the work environment.

- A start-up company / your own business – belonging to a group of like-minded individuals with similar aims and large dreams.

- Something else not listed here? Make a complete change, take a break from what you are doing now and redefine who you are and what you do?

3 Family

- Do you have a partner or family who need to be taken into account? Will they back any decision you want to take? Is there anything that they want or need from a change? Do you have to provide for anybody, and will that impact upon what you want to do?

You can only do exactly as you please either when there is only yourself to consider, or with the full support of those upon whom it will have an impact. In the majority of cases that impact will be upon our families, but often others are involved as well. We tend to build a pseudo family around us, including friends, partners and even neighbours and colleagues. If we want to make a change, they all need to be involved (preferably) or considered in the decision. It's no use going home one day and announcing that you have left one job and you are taking a sabbatical if your family are used to spending the money you earn or rely on it to live from day to day. Think about those people. How do the changes you make affect them? Moving to a new area can subject ourselves and our families to loneliness and a loss of support. When we disrupt that support network, we have to be prepared to help fill the void.

4 Resources

◆ Do you have access to the right resources? Do you have the time and the money you need? Do you have the technical equipment you need and access to the support needed if things go wrong? Internet access? Library access? Reliable transport?

Think about what resources you have that you can use to help you in deciding the There & Then for You plc. Then think about those resources you have that can help you get there. Think in terms of the following:

◆ **People.** Who do you know who can give you advice, act as a mentor, introduce you to alternative contacts or help you move into a new area?

◆ **Finance.** Are you financially independent? (You wish!) Are you able to take a drop in income, or can you gain an increase in income? What finances do you need to survive?

◆ **Time.** Can you afford to invest in yourself? Are you able to take the time to consider what you want to do and make sense of your own and others' needs?

◆ **Equipment/assets.** Computer? Mobile phone? Car?

5 Skills

◆ What skills have you identified? Do they enable you to make the changes you are considering? What new skills do you require? What will it take to obtain these skills? How will that impact upon location/family/values and lifestyle? Are there skills that you are not using? What could you do or be if you decided to use those? What qualifications do you want or need? How can you get them? What will getting them require (time, money, etc.)?

In Chapter 4 we asked you to list your skills and capabilities. Having done this you should reflect on them. Go back to see whether you are a specialist or a generalist. Do you use all of the skills you have now in your present role, and, if not, what skills do you have that can be used to either enhance your current position or to take you somewhere different?

How many ways could you use the skills you have defined? What sort of contacts and projects could you work on? What is the market value of these skills in the current marketplace? Are you getting the value that you could?

6 Finances

◆ What do you need to earn to be able to live each month? What are you paying for your mortgage? Do you have any savings? If you needed to raise money quickly, how would you do it and how much could you raise? Do you have to pay school fees? Are you expecting some large expenditure in the near future (moving home, building a conservatory, outstanding debt to clear, etc.)? How much will re-skilling cost?

It's no use making a change if the change we make cannot provide the financial support that is required. So, given the lifestyle you want, the family you have and the way you want to work, what is the realistic *minimum* earning level that you need to achieve?

EXERCISE

Review the headings and questions that we have given you here. Note that they are by no means comprehensive and that there will be more questions about these areas and other aspects of your life (e.g. spirituality) that you will need to ask yourself. Get some paper, or using the Your Notes page, draw a table like the one below and fill in all the columns. It should be a big page.

	What do you have now?	What do you want?	What would you give up?
Location			
Way of working			
Family			
Etc.			

Geoff's story

Geoff works for a large management consultancy group and is widely regarded as a thought leader in his particular field. He is so highly regarded that he is often asked to travel around the world to give presentations and seminars on his specialist area.

Yet Geoff is a corporate slave and has been for many years. He resigned from his previous company because he thought this new company would give him freedom and autonomy, but he has found that he's just swapped one set of constraints for another.

Geoff would love to escape and to become an independent free agent, and has been approached by a colleague keen to set up a small business. So why doesn't he go for it?

Geoff is divorced and has a child from this relationship. Because of the level of child maintenance that he is expected to pay each month he must have a guaranteed minimum level of income coming in to be able to meet the payments. Being an independent free agent may give him greater rewards over a period of time, but it doesn't give him the certainty that he needs. For Geoff it is this minimum level of earning that is the dominant factor in his career planning.

'There is nothing more difficult to carry out, nor more doubtful of success, nor more dangerous to handle, than to institute a new order of things.'

Machiavelli

Reality check

You need to consider all those areas listed above – they are all important. It's easy to say location is not an issue, but how many people do you know who return to areas they lived in before, particularly if it brings them closer to their families? If any of the questions here raise issues or obstacles that make you feel uneasy, take some time to think about them carefully. You need to recognize your limitations, even if they are not personal but environmental ones. It may stop you doing something stupid!

7 Values

How many of us hear stories of people like Geoff who move between organizations only to find that they don't fit in, or that they don't like the way the company does business?

This is often indicative of a mismatch in values between the individual and the organization they're working for. As a free agent, are you prepared to work in organizations that do not match your values and beliefs to make ends meet if necessary? Are you prepared to do a piece of work just for the money? At least as a free agent you can enter into situations of your own volition, knowing that it's temporary and that you can move on.

Alternatively, if you're a corporate person, do your values match those of your company? In *The Living Company,* Arie de Geus says that the foundation for Royal Dutch/Shell Group was a value system that had become a corporate constitution. He quotes from one corporate report:

'One company saw itself as a fleet of ships, each ship independent, yet the whole fleet stronger than the sum of its parts. This sense of belonging to an organization and being able to identify with its achievements can easily be dismissed as a soft or abstract feature of change. But case histories showed that strong employee links were essential for survival and change. Successful companies appear to maintain cohesion at all levels.'

Review your list of values and compare them to:

◆ those of the company you work for;

◆ the Chairman and/or Board of the company;

◆ your boss or Line Manager;

◆ your peers – the people you work with and who work for you.

Do they match? If not, start to list those companies and people you know who do share your values.

8 Belief

Your values are core to the essence of you and form the foundation of your belief system. We can say with a degree of certainty that, whilst this book will help you better understand your current position, it cannot guarantee that you will change. That is entirely down to your need and desire for change and, ultimately, your *belief* that change is not only possible, but what *you* want.

'What counts is not necessarily the size of the dog in the fight – it's the size of the fight in the dog.'

Dwight D. Eisenhower

If you really want to get out of life what you are putting in, then you must have the self-confidence and self-belief to know that it is possible.

Reality check

This does not mean arrogance. We are talking about having confidence and belief based on robust self-awareness.

The best presenters and the best trainers are not necessarily the ones who have the best slide shows. They are the ones who know their subject so well that they don't have to read it out from a book or a script. They are the ones who are so passionate about their subject that you know that they really believe in what they're saying.

Start by getting passionate about yourself and believing that you are capable of great things!

For a while neither of us really believed that we could write and publish a book, but by sticking with it, and Gary beating Stuart around the head with blunt instruments to get him to do the work, we did it. The main reason that we were able to achieve this was because we knew we could rely on each other to be positive and proactive. If you want to make a change that sticks, *hang around with positive people!* Negative people get negative results, if they get any results at all. Hanging around with negative people will give you a negative attitude too. Trust us. We've been there – don't do it!

NASA story

There is a famous story about the visit of a former President of the United States of America to the NASA Space Programme. As he walked around the site he was shown into an enormous hangar where the Apollo spacecraft were prepared for launching. In one corner of the hangar was a janitor, meticulously sweeping the polished floor.

The President decided that this was a good opportunity to demonstrate 'the common touch' and so he approached the janitor. The President asked the janitor: 'What are you doing here?' The janitor stopped his sweeping, looked at the President and said: 'I am helping to put our astronauts into space.'

Just in case you miss the significance of this, it is absolutely vital that floors in space hangars are kept spotlessly clean so that any drops of oil, lubricant, etc. that might signify a leak, or any dropped screws, bolts, tools, etc., can be spotted quickly and easily.

In this case someone had done an excellent job of explaining to the janitor the essential nature of his occupation, its importance and therefore *his* importance. We think that it would be great to be doing something that made us feel that important, something that we believed in so totally. What do you think?

Are there limitations to what you want to achieve?

In the future your career will not just end. The theme here is life-long learning and payment for the accumulated skills you can market to the clients that need them. *Age is no longer the issue that it once was.* We should all be aiming a little higher and further than early retirement. Why not have future goals and development needs so that at the end of our corporate employment phase we don't fall into an abyss, asking ourselves 'what's next?' or 'is that it?'

Think about the limitations that we impose upon ourselves, or society tries to impose upon us. Don't think about what you want to achieve as being limited to an age 55, 60 or 65. Think about what you would really like to do and ask yourself: 'Is that something I could do when I retire?' For example: you may have an interest in the History of Art and, whilst you can go to night school to learn more about it, you are frustrated that you cannot give more time to it. What is to stop you going to university to study History of Art when you retire? What is to stop you volunteering to work part-time somewhere which gives you access to art?

EXERCISE

Go back to your list of areas to be considered in your There & Then (location, family, finances, etc.) and think about the limitations that you have now which will not be there in the future. Think about things that you could do if, for example, you retire at 60 knowing that your life expectancy is 80.

YOUR NOTES

What career elements do you need?

What would be your dream job? Go on – if you could be anything, what would it be?

It's strange but many people don't have a clue what to say to this, and, if pushed, pick a job that exists higher up where they already work. Oh, please! This shows that they're just thinking within their own little box, limiting their horizons. Use your imagination! Come out of the box for a while!

How can we remove the boxes?

The first task is to remove these blockages to your thinking and take a wider look at what you want from a role and your career by not thinking about what you do now. In Chapter 4 you identified your transferable skills, talents and experiences. The majority of these skills are not necessarily constrained to the role you are doing now.

EXERCISE

Go back and review your skill audit.

Are there any skills there that you really enjoy using but don't use to do your job? What are they, why are they important and why aren't you doing a job that does make use of them?

Okay, pay attention, key message now:

The 'There & Then' that you are trying to identify does *not* consist of one job or role; it is made up of a number of key elements that are important to you and which reflect your lifestyle requirements.

Any job or role, even your dream job, consists of a number of basic *elements* that constitute its whole. If you look at your current job, you should be able to break it down to show how it is made up: what skills you use, what way of working you have to follow, and so on. If you break down your dream job into these elements, it can help you to define what is important for you in any future role.

We compare this to the process you will go through when looking to buy a new house. When we start looking at everything that's available we quickly filter out a lot of the houses that we're sent for consideration. We do this by thinking of the key *elements* of what we are looking for, and bear in mind our ideal dream home. This gives us a yardstick by which to measure new properties we see. Of course, the chances of finding something perfect are, at best, slim, so we set ourselves an *acceptance level* where a house contains, say, 7 out of the 10 things we're looking for. We only go to see it if it passes that acceptance level. We also prioritize our elements so that if we have to compromise, we know what we'll be prepared to give up and what we won't. We also start to see negative things that we want to avoid.

For example, we might want an old detached house with a garage and three bedrooms, within walking distance of a school and with good commuter links, in a quiet neighbourhood with a reasonable-size garden. We can quickly filter out anything without parking, and avoid anything on a modern estate, etc., etc.

You should be able to apply this in just the same way to your There & Then. Define a set of elements for your future career development, based on what your dream job would be. Your dream job may seem ridiculous, but think of 10 elements that attract you to it, and if you can find a real job or role that gives you a score of 8 out of 10, that is pretty damn close to achieving it!

This exercise can have another purpose – if you take the time to break your dream job down into its component elements robustly and honestly, you'll probably see that it's not really as attractive as you thought. You might only be attracted to one or two elements of that job and it might be that you wouldn't actually be very happy doing it at all.

If we concentrate on the key elements we want from a role or career, we can remove the box from our current thinking. If you are a specialist, then use this exercise within the constraints of the boundaries of your field to find promotion opportunities, alternative companies, a way of using your specialized skill in other areas of interest. Looking at individual elements enables you to concentrate on your skills and talents without confining you to a given role, business or industry.

What sorts of career elements are there?

Probably as many as you want, but here are some categories you might wish to consider:

- **Control.** Do you want to be in charge or are you happy to follow?

- **Time.** How many hours are you happy devoting to your work?

- **Creativity.** Are you happy following rules, or do you want to colour outside the lines?

- **Managing.** Do you enjoy looking after people and making things happen through them?

- **Location.** Where do you want to live and work? The suburbs? The city? The country? Independent of a particular location?

- **Responsibility.** Do you want to be making the 'big' decisions?

- **Specialization.** Do you want to become a specialist in a given field and be respected for that? Or do you want to be a generalist?

- **Flexibility.** Do you require a 9-to-5 role, or are you happy with putting the hours in and taking them back as and when?

- **Company.** Do you want to associate with a company? Or with several particular types of companies? Do you want to be a complete free agent?

- **Skills.** Do you want to use your current skills? Or do you want to develop in a new and to you more exciting area?

- **Belonging.** Do you need to belong to a group and make connections with people? Are you happy moving quickly from project to project making very little emotional attachment with people and companies you work for?

Write down your answers again – they are important!

By concentrating on the elements that we wish to satisfy, as opposed to the role we currently have, we open up our thinking beyond the box in which we currently sit. We highlight new areas, perhaps areas that we hadn't considered working in before.

Andy's story

Andy is 35 and is a Web Designer currently employed on a fixed-term two-year contract for a major corporation. He enjoys the work but feels that the role is constraining him and failing to enlarge his skills. The company is relying on Andy for his expertise, but it doesn't help train him, enhance his capabilities or consider him within its own development system (the price of being a free agent for Andy).

Andy has worked previously with a number of clients and has a good network of contacts within the industry. In the long term he thinks he wants to be a project manager as opposed to only a Web Designer.

When asked to do the element analysis exercise, Andy came up with the following immediate career elements:

- Avoid working in a large organization that isolates contractors from their own people.

- Manage web marketing projects from inception to delivery.

- Work on marketing aspects of the internet and become a known market expert on the use of web-based marketing.

- Work on more short-term contracts over the next two years.

- Act as a talent scout for Web Designers as opposed to being a Web Designer.

- Move to a less office-based environment – to home-based or leased office arrangement.

- Have project management-based skills.

- Develop a virtual company based on the following expert areas – web design, web marketing and project management of web marketing projects.

These are the elements that Andy wants to look for. This enables him to start planning his immediate future, i.e. the next few months, and his focus for the next two years. Andy will have to either disconnect himself from the current company he's working for, even perhaps to the extent of arranging his own replacement, or he can complete his contract whilst using his own time to develop his future strategy, build his network and identify alternative opportunities.

As Andy starts to think out of the box, it may lead him in a slightly different direction – maybe to start a contracting business finding work for other Web Designers as they move towards project management.

Andy has opted to give himself more time and start doing the groundwork whilst still working for the same company.

By focusing on individual elements, you can determine whether your actions are moving you towards the right career or away from it. In defining your ideal role elements, you have to be aware that the time-scales to make the changes will vary depending on what you are aiming for. Remember that you will not be able to achieve a

10 out of 10 immediately and that there will always be a price to pay as you move from where you are now to where you want to be. *The journey begins with a first step, not a giant leap.*

EXERCISE

Think through what your dream career or role will consist of, in terms of the elements you wish it to have.

Base this on your past experiences, skills and needs.

Don't be afraid of putting anything down – everybody has dreams of things that they want to do, of who they want to be and of what they want their lives to look like. Why not you?

If you have trouble doing this, take some time to consider your results from Chapter 4. When you look at the person you defined there, what sort of elements do you think will be important to them? What sort of future would suit them?

The aim of this is to draw up a list of the elements in a career that you want, elements that will enable you to feel fulfilled, motivated, happy and challenged.

Reality check

If you're still eyeing up your boss's job, then we would suggest that you go out and do something amazing! Come back to this book after you've swum with dolphins, run with the bulls at Pamplona and insulted your boss at least once. Perhaps then you can start to believe in all that you can be and all that you are capable of.

Without imagination you will never come close to realizing your potential.

Your dream role consists of the key elements you identified above. By breaking it down into its component parts you have started to formulate:

1 whether it is achievable;

2 what the skill gaps are between what you have now and what you would need to achieve your dream;

3 what the most important elements are to you.

EXERCISE

Repeat the previous exercise, but this time think about what your absolute worst nightmare job would be (e.g. working in an abattoir or anything with lots of bureaucracy).

Again, what are the elements that make up this job, and which ones can you therefore identify as the ones you want to avoid?

Your dream job may be unattainable because you are unable to gain one of the key skills, but *do not* despair! By looking at the elements you have identified of your dream job you may be able to identify another career path that will enable you to meet the majority of these elements and which may give you every bit as much satisfaction.

Vision

You need a vision and a mission

We know that for some of you this will be a novel idea, and others will be sick to death of mission statements. But most companies that use them devise them, print them on a card, put them on a wall, then ignore them or forget about them. The reason that these vision and mission statements usually fail is that the company only ever talks-the-talk. If the senior managers who issued a vision statement truly believed it, they would be living it, be enthused and passionate about it, wanting to get everyone else to buy into it. When was the last time your boss talked to you about the corporate vision with anything approaching enthusiasm?

When used properly and believed in, vision and missions can be incredibly powerful. A student at university training to be a physiotherapist has a vision of being a qualified, certified physiotherapist. Every time they have a bad day or feel bogged down reading in the library, that vision spurs them on. Their personal There & Then is defined in just a few short words. You need to be able to do this too, to have a one-liner that you can repeat to yourself every time the going gets a bit tough. Without one, you lose focus and soon start drifting without direction again.

As the old story goes: There are three builders working on a building. A visitor asks each of them what they are doing. The first replies that he is laying bricks. The second states he is building a wall. The third builder tells the visitor with passion, 'Me, I'm building a cathedral.' *Are you building a cathedral or just laying bricks?*

Every day you must contribute to your future and act within your beliefs and values. Your own Personal Mission Statement should look forward and be indicative of what you want to be and where you want to go. Stephen Covey calls this *'beginning with the end in mind'* (*7 Habits of Highly Effective People*). If you are thinking 'Where do I start with this?', bear in mind that you already have!

Don't restrict yourself to work. Your vision should include:

◆ who you want to be;

◆ how you will look;

◆ what you will be wearing;

◆ where you will be;

◆ who will be with you;

◆ what your home will look like;

◆ how it will smell;

◆ how it will be decorated;

- what your work will look like;
- what role you will have there.

EXERCISE

Sit down and take some time. You know who you are and have started to define what you want.

Think about the information you have so far, prioritize it and write down what you want to achieve, how you want to achieve it and how you want to do it.

Look at what you have written. Can you believe it? Does it make your heart soar? Does it make you passionate about making the change happen? Revise it, shorten it and make it come alive.

When you are happy with it, write it up and keep it where you can find it and look at it every day.

Direction, speed planning and career actions

Direction: which way do you want to develop?

As a free agent, you can't rely on your current market always being there. Companies, industries and markets move, change and alter focus, as do the skills and products they require. By being aware of the environment and 'prairie-dogging', you can be aware of what change is taking place and how best to develop You as a company in response to the changes.

One way to ensure that you develop in the most appropriate way or where your skills are most applicable is by thinking about markets using *Ansoff's Matrix* (Figure 6.1), which considers the interaction of skills and markets.

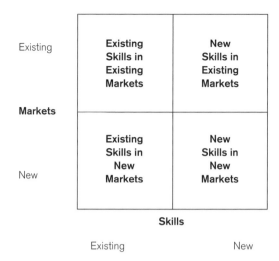

	Existing	New
Existing	**Existing Skills in Existing Markets**	**New Skills in Existing Markets**
Markets		
New	**Existing Skills in New Markets**	**New Skills in New Markets**

Skills

Existing   New

Figure 6.1 *Ansoff's Matrix*

You can develop by applying both your existing skills and new ones in both existing and new markets. A description of each sector is given below.

◆ **Existing skills in existing markets.** This represents a market with low risk and little need for skills growth and represents an area of stability. However, this area is shrinking in the current environment due to the changing nature of work where companies cannot guarantee 'jobs for life'. In the future this represents moving between businesses or projects that are familiar and rely on the same skill set.

◆ **Existing skills in new markets.** This is a low-risk area that represents the reinvention of skills in an emerging market. General skills are applied till the market matures and starts to demand specific skills. This means you are able to move early into the market with your current skill base and stay with it until your skills and those of the business become divergent. At the stage that the market changes, if you wish to stay here, it may be necessary to invest in certain additional skill sets.

◆ **New skills in existing markets.** Having invested time and energy in new skills, you are able to put them to use in your existing market and change your position and worth. A good example of this is company sponsorship on MBA courses. This gives the individual new skills and can result in them being promoted into new areas of the company to use these accumulated skills. Often this approach is prompted through internal development programmes, internal company requirements and driven by technology changes.

◆ **New skills in new markets.** This is a far riskier permutation that is often determined by changes in market and technology. Often this requires the individual to recognize the need for a complete career change prompted by an examination of lifestyle and values or external forces – corporate re-engineering, redundancy. However, it can also occur when an individual has entrepreneurial instincts and decides they want to go it alone, taking the chance that they can make it or having a fallback that their current skills will guarantee them a position if their plan fails.

It may be that you need to develop new skills, new markets or a combination of the two to achieve your There & Then. This will mean you being prepared to adopt a much riskier development strategy. If you choose this option, be sure that you have thought carefully about the price that you might have to pay if it does not work out.

EXERCISE

Draw Ansoff's Matrix on a blank piece of paper and write in your skills with markets that you could enter. See where you are positioned now and where you are heading.

Once you have done this you will be able to consider the strategy you wish to adopt for your development, based on whether your goals are orientated to existing markets and skills or the development of new skills and moves towards newer and emerging markets.

Speed planning: step size

When mapped out, we see that moving towards our development goals can be seen as a series of steps. Any development action will be a step forward, but step size will vary. The step change can be large or small.

◆ **Large steps.** When we wish to change the nature of the game and improve or step towards our goal in large strides. For example, studying for a professional qualification in a new area.

◆ **Small steps.** The everyday improvements and changes that over a long period move us forward in ways that may not be readily discernible to the naked eye yet are the result of constant application and drive. For example, the day-to-day application of a new skill to embed it, or asking peers for feedback to update your self-awareness constantly.

In most cases the goals can be divided into those that require a large step change and those that can be achieved by lots of small steps in the direction we wish to go.

For example, here are two development goals that have been set:

◆ to improve report layout and design to better suit the target customer;

◆ to improve report writing skills.

If we look at the step size required for these development activities they could be determined thus:

- ◆ **Improving layout.** Large step change required. Attend workshop on report writing and layout. Purchase higher specification word processing software package and implement standard report template.

- ◆ **Improving writing skills.** Small step change. Review carefully previous reports and the language they contained. Discuss different ways of presenting information and the language used. Test theories by rewriting reports for new emphasis and have new versions reviewed by peers.

In this case, to change and improve the layout of our reports may require an external intervention or influence. This ensures a step change in our ability from our current level. However, to improve our writing skills can be achieved by day-to-day activities and by focusing on this skill.

Having your development goals defined is one thing. The determination of the scale of the change you wish to make is another. Only you can determine the type of step you wish to take based on your own development options, needs and most suitable learning style.

There is, of course, another option. If report writing really is a weakness for you and if you have something to offer in return, why not identify someone else who does it well and ask that they take on board reviewing and editing all your reports?

Career actions

During your career any action you take can be categorized under one of ten options. Each option describes an action that can be taken at any time, according to your development or lifestyle needs. The ten actions are as follows:

1 **Stationary.** When, after analysis, you realize that your current role suits your needs and current development requirements. There is therefore no need to focus on other areas, but do focus on developing the skills suited to your needs and the needs of the role.

2 **Enrichment.** Noting that the current role is completed with reasonable ease, that the role is acceptable but that you need additional challenges within that role (e.g. by adding tasks and responsibilities to those presently held, expanding your current role to retain motivation and add greater value to the business).

3 **Exploration.** With the realization that staying in the current role would result in the loss of motivation and limited room for expansion, you might be unsure of what to do next. You decide to experience working in other roles, but without seeking full-time change or a new role. This is often easier in large corporations, where project work, interim management and shadowing are available or simpler to arrange. It often requires your superior to notice that you're stagnating in your current role.

4 **Lateral.** Having ascertained where you wish to go to in the long term, the gap analysis conducted indicates that there is a mismatch between skills and experience and long-term aims. However, there is no easy way of attaining those skills from the current position or obtaining the relevant training. The action is to move sideways, accepting a delay in the career path, whilst accumulating the skills to make the next step.

5 **Promotion.** Having outgrown the current role and assessed the enrichment, exploration and lateral actions, the only way forward from the current position is to seek promotion. This avenue is also appropriate when individuals are looking for increased rewards for individual efforts. Promotion can be within the current company or to an external company demanding the same skills and experience.

6 **Downshifting.** (Often taken as a lifestyle choice.) By deciding to take less work responsibility and pressure, you exchange salary, influence and standing so that you can concentrate on other facets of your life outside work. People often opt for this when they have attained a level of savings and income that removes their dependence on a high salary. This can be possible within a current company, or moving to an external company that has a suitable role and is willing to accept that the individual will not

be seeking promotion. It can sometimes be seen in a high-level individual wishing to take on a consultancy or part-time role.

7   Relocating. Very much a lifestyle choice relying on obtaining a position using current skills, but deciding that there would be a better quality of life by using them in a different geographical location. You may need to accept that this could result in a reduced income, e.g. moving from employment in a large city to a more rural area.

8   Redirecting. Similar in nature to the lateral action. The aim here is to use employment to change focus completely: that is, not to accumulate additional skills but to change the skill set completely. It will often result in the need to accept a reduction in income and is, therefore, often a lifestyle choice based on your values and needs.

9   Proposing. Particularly in companies that experience high growth rates or high degrees of change, new roles and responsibilities can be discovered or defined as they occur. This results in you being able to propose a new role, new work and/or new responsibilities from your current role, discussing changes in remuneration and status as appropriate.

10   External. A realization that within current employment, your values, needs and aspirations and those of the company are different. This leads to you seeking a change of employer or seeking to run your own business or free agency.

Taking all the information you have gathered so far, you can now decide which of the actions best suits your current needs. Your decision will need to reflect your values, needs and vision. It's your choice.

EXERCISE

Look at where you are now. What actions will help you get to where you want to go?

Plot the moves you need to make and the advantages and disadvantages of each. What is the first step, the one that will start the process?

YOUR NOTES

Goal setting

So it's time to start moving! It's time to set out your objectives by comparing your results from the Here & Now tools to those you have from the There & Then tools. What you are looking for are the gaps that need closing, the Bridge that you need to build to get you from Here & Now to There & Then.

The goals that you will set will be appropriate to where *you* want to go and how *you* can bridge your gap. As you set the goals that you want to achieve, both short-term and long-term, we would ask you to remember two words – **SMART** and **IDEAL**:

SMART

◆ **S**pecific – Related to a particular action.

◆ **M**easurable – You should be able to measure when the goals have been attained.

◆ **A**chievable – It should be within your circle of influence to reach the goals.

◆ **R**ealistic – Don't have goals that are out of reach. It's really disconcerting if you never reach any of them.

◆ **T**imely – Goals are able to be completed in a given time-frame.

IDEAL

◆ **I**nspirational – Your vision should be what motivates you, drives you, inspires you.

◆ **D**efined – You have a clearly defined There & Then that you are going to achieve. Your goals must also be defined as thoroughly as possible.

- ◆ **E**nergizing – Goal setting makes it real, and that should give you the feeling that even at three in the morning you want to be working on your goals.

- ◆ **A**spirational – Your goals close a gap between where you are now and what you aspire to be.

- ◆ **L**eading – Your vision, and therefore the goals that help you build towards that vision, should be strong enough to drive the way you behave.

However, one thing to remember …

Reality check on goals

A lecturer stands at the front of a class and proceeds to take a jar and fill it with different sized stones. First he puts in some large stones and then asks the class if the jar is full. The answer they give is 'no', so he proceeds to add smaller stones, filling the gaps around the large stones. Again he asks if the jar is full, and, at the answer 'no', proceeds to add tiny stones and eventually sand. The jar now appears full and again he asks the question, 'Is the jar full?' Some now answer 'yes', some hesitate and some say 'no'. The lecturer takes the jar to a tap, where he adds water, filling the jar to the brim.

With the jar full, he asks the class: 'If the jar represented the time available to you to achieve your goals, what is the lesson you can learn from this?' Almost to a person they each reply that no matter how full your life seems, you can always create room to do more. The lecturer states that this is not the lesson he wants the students to learn. Perplexed, they ask him what the lesson is.

The lesson, he says, is: 'Always remember to get the big things in first.'

Remember, as you plan your goals, get the big ones in first.

EXERCISE

Look at Here & Now. Look at There & Then. Identify the gaps.

Relate these to your vision and start to map out the steps that you need to take.

Which are big steps, and which are the little ones?

Prioritize them.

Start to plan how to build the Bridge.

Write it down.

YOUR NOTES

Brand management

What does your brand look like?

In the free agent world, brand is everything: it represents who you are, the work you do and determines your reputation amongst colleagues, clients, associates and in the markets in which you work. Work is all about reputation. It is about how you are regarded by your clients – your professionalism, as much as the results you create for them. Think about your colleagues who are busy, or who have the reputation for always bringing in work. Why is that? It's because they are managing their clients, and they can do this because the clients think highly of them. In some cases they will be offering some specialist skill or knowledge that the clients want or need but in other cases they will offer nothing except an air of confidence. They are no better than you, but they project themselves in such a way that clients see them and think 'professional'. They are living a brand.

The same is true if you are a company worker. Customer views on your performance, 360° feedback, internal client satisfaction reports – these are all brand measurements. They represent how you and your brand are being received and what impact it is having.

What brand do you want?

Every brand has an image. What do you want yours to be? What do you want people to think when they look at you, talk to you or meet you?

Do you want to be a luxury item – a Rolex watch? Refined with years of experience in your field, something that is relied upon day after day, year after year, to operate without a problem. Or do you see yourself as a Swatch watch? Ever-changing the way it looks and the methods it uses to produce the same result. To always be changing to suit the environment, coming out with new features and innovative ideas that maintain your level of lifestyle. If we align careers to these two products, the career paths will be very different. Two different brands appealing to different markets and different companies.

Whilst one brand is suited to more traditional industries, long associations and long-term results, the other demands quick changes, never standing still in one place for long enough to settle, but producing the results required for the time it is used. You need to determine what sort of brand you have or you want to have.

Jo's story

As an Independent Consultant, Jo had stopped working directly for companies in order to live a different brand. Out went the business suits and smart dressing and in came a more casual approach. At the first client meetings she wore smart business wear, but after that she dressed casually. She believed in the material she was delivering, not the look of the presenter.

However, after several engagements, the review sheets indicated a particular theme:

◆ 'Not professionally presented.'

◆ 'Whilst the content is excellent, I am not sure that this is appropriate for our corporate environment.'

◆ 'Not happy with method of presentation.'

After being asked some more questions, the clients revealed that they could not connect the image being portrayed with the content of the training. The content of the course was considered entirely appropriate to the delegates' needs and was considered thoroughly worthwhile, but because it was delivered in a casual and laid-back manner, it was out of step with the corporate world in which it was being delivered.

The brand Jo was using, whilst suiting her personally, was out of step with the marketplace in which it was being delivered. Jo altered her image and the change of client perception was immediate. The clients' reservations disappeared and they were happy with the course.

As you think about your future, you need to think about your brand, and, in doing this, there are four areas that you need to consider. These are:

1 Product.

2 Price.

3 Placement.

4 Promotion.

These are the same as the considerations given to any item or service that is sold.

1 Product: What are you selling?

Look at your skill set and values and ask yourself: what product does this encapsulate?

Think of it this way: if you were a car, what would you be?

◆ A Ferrari – fast, sleek and expensive to run.

◆ A Mini – small, compact and stylish. Cheap to run and nimble to manoeuvre.

◆ An Edsel – obsolescent and in the garage, a collectors' item, but regarded as no use to the market.

◆ A Lexus – efficient and stylish, cost-effective with prestige.

EXERCISE

Make a note of what sort of car you think you are now and how you think others perceive you. Go and ask others for their opinion and feedback.

Now look at There & Then and your vision. What sort of car are you looking at now, and is it different to the one you see in Here & Now? Is that person different to the one you are perceived as at the moment?

2   Price: How much is it worth?

Is it a luxury good that demands a premium price, or something that is a generic item that has a price reflected in order to sell it in sufficient volume? Knowing these two factors leads you to identify how best to position your brand in the marketplace.

Your position in the marketplace has a huge bearing on skills you have, the skills you need and in determining the price you can get. We can represent this very simply as in Figure 6.2.

Figure 6.2 *Skill level versus price matrix*

- A Premium product – exclusive, high skill level demanding high cost.

- A Mass product – a low skill level and thus low cost.

- A Relationship product – relies on networking and contacts to gain a premium on a low skill level.

- A Time Served product – requires high skill but is now not wanted in the marketplace and thus only demands a low price.

EXERCISE

Think about what you offer now. Is this what you want to continue to do, or do you want to move into another, high earning, sector?

If you want to change, what does this mean for your skill set, your vision and your There & Then?

---

3 Placement: Where is it being sold?

Is the product being sold exactly where we would expect to find it? Is it a high-class boutique, full of new and innovative items, or are we in the bargain basement?

EXERCISE

Where are your skills being sold at the moment? Where would be the best place to sell your There & Then? Do the two match? If not, have you built this into your vision? Do it now – it needs to be part of the There & Then.

4 Promotion: How is it being advertised?

What makes it different to anything else in that area of the market? What is unique about it? What added value can it bring and how can it be made to stand out from the rest? What is there about it that will attract potential clients to this product before any others? What is its USP (unique selling point)?

> **EXERCISE**
>
> Ask colleagues about the image that you portray. Does this fit with your There & Then? What does You plc look like when it goes to market – what is it dressed in, how does it behave? Write it down. Add it to There & Then.

The steps that you can take to move into a new market area or income stream can be affected, proactively, by altering your image. By identifying your specialism and marketing it properly, you can move from a commodity product to a premium or niche product! It's simply *Putting you the Product in the right Place at the right Price and dressing it up to Promote it properly.*

> **EXERCISE**
>
> Take some time and reflect on You plc. Where are you as a brand now? Write down the current state of your brand, asking yourself the following questions:
>
> ◆ What type of product do you want to be? High skill level and high margin? A mass consumer brand, able to work in any environment with generic skills? How can your skills identified in the Here & Now be marketed? What area best suits them?

- What image do you want your brand to have? Is it a suit? Is it a tee shirt and jeans? Or are you able to dress like a nerd because your product is so in demand at the present time? What will your clients expect to see?

- What skills do you require in the current environment? Is this a boom time? Is this a bust time? Have you an area of expertise that can be developed into a premium product, or should you look to develop wider skills to ride out the bad times more easily?

- Where do you want that brand positioned: do you want to be a big fish in a small pond or a small fish in a big pond? Or ultimately as your own brand – the free agent.

Having written down your brand as it is now, write down what you want it to be (within sensible limits – you know what you are and are not capable of achieving). Use your Here & Now information on your values, skills and what others think of you to build the new brand for You plc.

If we can decide what type of product and brand we want to be, we can look at supporting this brand by training, image, behaviour, branding and promotion, the important thing being to note that you have to live it. It has to match your values.

What are your elevator pitch, business card and strapline?

Imagine you're in a lift and somewhere between the tenth floor and the ground floor you find that you have the chance to pitch for some work, an engagement or even just introduce yourself. At the end of that pitch you hand over your business card. What do you say? What's your pitch? What does your card say and how does it say it? Remember what we have said about managing your own reputation and ask yourself: 'What is my approach to selling myself and what should it be for You plc?'

The business card reflects your attitude towards work, gives contact information and reflects who you are simply by the quality of the paper, the typefaces used, the use and type of colours, the logo (if any), the layout and the use of a 'strapline'. The 'strapline' concept is like a headline – it's the heading you see on the front of the newspaper that catches your eye and gets you to buy it.

EXERCISE

Sit back and envisage the business card and strapline for You plc. Draw what it looks like, what it states about you and what you can do.

Reality check

Branding can be great fun because it's an opportunity to let rip and use your imagination, but it can be an area that's fraught with danger. Be aware that something that you find funny or interesting may cause offence to some people. Stay away from anything that might be open to ambiguity or that might cause distress in any part of the community. Check with others if you're not sure about anything.

Mary's story: a cautionary tale

Mary is a successful Independent Trainer, running her own business. The training she delivers is largely based on a number of books that she has written. All of the training interventions rely on a range of media to help get messages across and reinforce them. The training courses Mary runs are very well received and are widely considered a great deal of fun by delegates.

Recently Mary took one of her products to a new client, a large, old-fashioned company with an extremely professional reputation. Mary was asked to deliver one of her three-day courses on a specific subject on the understanding that, if it were well received, more courses would follow.

The course was delivered and appeared to go very well, until a few days later when Mary received a call from the company informing her that there had been a complaint about one of the video clips used during the course. The clip in question was from *When Harry Met Sally* and was the famous scene in which Meg Ryan, playing Sally, demonstrates how some women may fake the amount of enjoyment they get from sex. Mary was told that this clip had caused offence to one of the delegates and that it would have to be removed from the course if Mary were to deliver it to the company again.

Think about anything that could offend anyone, be deemed 'inappropriate' or damage your reputation.

YOUR NOTES

07

chapter seven
so what?

Recap

Here's where you should be by now:

Firstly, from Here & Now you should have a snapshot of what You plc looks like at this moment in time, including:

- a picture of the job you have now and the level of responsibility that you have;

- a picture of your lifestyle, who and what is important to you away from work;

- a skills audit, including your experience and capabilities;

- an idea of your value system;

- a greater awareness of the environment beyond your immediate surroundings;

- an idea of what other people think of you.

Important note

As there is a lot of information here, take the time to condense it down into, if possible, no more than two sheets of A4 paper.

Secondly, you should have spent some time 'dreaming with structure', looking to the future, identifying what you want to achieve and when you want to get there by: your own There & Then, including:

- a picture of your future lifestyle;

- a list of the elements that it's important for you to include in any job or role that you have in the future;

- a list of those elements you do *not* want in your future;

- a personal brand for You plc that you're going to start living day-to-day;

- a vision and a mission statement;

- some goals for yourself, both short- and long-term.

> **Important note**
> Again, try to condense all of this information down into no more than two sheets of A4 paper.

Starting planning

By now, the key word is *planning*. Remember the 6P's: Prior Preparation and Planning Prevent Poor Performance!

Before we get stuck into building the Bridge from Here & Now to There & Then, we need to be sure that we are building with the right materials. So, before we go rushing out to do something, let's make sure that it is really going to help (by achieving one of our key elements, or by identifying possible pitfalls along the way). Detailed planning will help us to identify the price we might have to pay to get there.

Start by sitting down with Here & Now on your left and There & Then on your right. Look at them. Compare them. Identify the gaps. Identify the similarities. Identify the opportunities. Identify the strengths.

You need to know what skills you already have that can be used as stepping stones, and you need to know those areas that you have to be prepared to invest in to build the right skill set. Be robust and honest!

What is the level of change you want to make?

When building the There & Then, you might have seen a pattern emerging that has led you to think:

◆ The job and lifestyle that I have is the right one for me. I don't need to make any changes.

Or

◆ I only need to make some small changes to get me there. Fine tuning is all that is required.

Or

◆ I can see that the person that I am describing in There & Then would be perfectly suited to a job in, let's say, marketing, or perhaps doing what I am doing now but as an independent consultant.

Or

◆ I can see that I am in completely the wrong area and need to make a big change in my life if I am to be happy and motivated.

1   **No changes required.** Good. This is not unusual. We have both had experiences of going and looking at other opportunities and coming away with the feeling that, actually, we are better off where we are. If, through the exercises in this book, you have realized that you are in the right place, right now, then that should mean that tomorrow you can go to work feeling happier, more motivated and ready to use these tools to make you more successful.

2   **Small changes.** That must be great – knowing that you are so close. Our one suggestion would be that, however close you think you are, make sure that you plan out those few steps carefully – don't rush it! If you are that close, you will be there soon enough, so make sure that you get there safely and fully equipped.

3   **Perfectly suited.** This can be as dangerous as it can be inspiring. Inspiring to be able to identify what you should do or what area to go into, and so having something to focus on. Dangerous in that you need to double-check this carefully before doing anything. It may be that you have subconsciously geared all your exercises to come up with an answer you have vaguely had in mind all along. If you've always thought you should work in marketing, for example, you might have created a There & Then that reflects what you imagine a career in marketing should look like. You need to check this before you start implementing changes.

4 **Big change needed.** This can be very daunting. At this point it is important to remember that the big change starts with a small step – don't panic and don't worry. In this chapter we will introduce you to a tool which will help you break this big leap down into lots of small steps.

Of course, for some of you, you will look at your There & Then and not see any of these themes. You might be looking at it and thinking: 'I can't see any job or role or business that will give me what I want!' That is okay. Here's what you need to do:

◆ Start by looking at the elements that you have identified and have a think about friends, colleagues, associates, etc., who are in jobs that match some or all of those skills.

◆ Look at the elements that you have identified and cluster them, put them together into small groups, and consider how you can address each group. Remember: the There & Then is not necessarily about one job or role! It may be that a number of the elements can be satisfied by a particular job whilst the remainder are satisfied either by getting a second job or role, or by pursuing other interests away from work (through study, hobbies, clubs, societies, community or charity roles).

Remember
This is not just about the job or career – it's about your life and your values. You need to research your There & Then thoroughly – you need to know about the industry, the role and the company that you might be working in. Go to your local business library or to a careers office and have a look at them. These establishments always have career guidebooks that give an introduction to many different industries and roles. Of course, much of this information is now available on the internet, so you could do it at home or in your local internet café. There's no excuse for ignorance these days!

Say you want to get into Marketing. Fine. However, there are an awful lot of very different Marketing companies out there, in different locations, looking at different things, working in different ways. You have to go and find the company or environment that fits with You plc in your There & Then. Be picky.

Testing the change

You might now have got to a point where you have identified one or more options that may, or may not, help Bridge the gap to There & Then. At this point we need to think about doing some serious testing to make sure that the option we take is the right one.

Testing should be done in two stages:

1   High-level.

2   Detailed.

1   High-level

EXERCISE

Looking at the job description and, if appropriate, the details of the company you might be working for, compare these to Here & Now and There & Then. On a piece of paper list the key, high-level, positive and negative points about taking the job.

For example, if we were considering a move into Sales, we might consider the following:

Positives	Negatives
Managerial skills	No Sales experience
Line Manager reference	Limited mobility
Energy, ambition, interest	Limited contacts in Sales
Knowledge of the product	Other reactions
Knowledge of the industry	Current job important
Dealing with customers	Time away from home and family
Computer literate	
Driver	
Look the part	
Desire to learn	

(This is a simplified version of Kurt Lewin's *Force Field Analysis*, published in 1947.)

Doing this as a quick and ready planning aid should bring out the key points based on your gut instinct. It needs to give a good overview of the implications of the change you are thinking of making. When you do this it may become clear that there are one or more dominant factor(s), something that is so important to your values that it overrides all other considerations.

Sarah's story

Sarah was working for a large public company and was heavily involved in the design and delivery of training. She enjoyed her work but was frustrated by the endless bureaucracy and the knowledge that, as a competent trainer, she could earn a lot more money working either independently or for another business.

An old friend of Sarah's was working for a small, well-established training company delivering training to sales staff and was happy to introduce Sarah to the business. Sarah sent in a CV and was invited to meet the Managing Director. The interview went well and Sarah was then invited to go through a formal recruitment process. She went for it.

On the surface the job was excellent:

◆ Pure training design and delivery.

◆ Less bureaucratic business.

◆ Well-established – good customer base.

◆ Head office located just a short drive from her home.

◆ Much higher salary.

◆ Good bonus scheme.

◆ Excellent car.

What more could she want?

The recruitment process was challenging, but Sarah enjoyed that, and prepared for each stage thoroughly, including her own list of searching questions to ask. By the time Sarah reached the final interview she felt that she had a very robust picture of what the company was about and felt that she really wanted to work for them.

At the final interview she asked a question about how much time staff spent travelling and away from home and she was dismayed by the answer. One of the trainers had calculated that in the previous year he had spent over three weeks sitting in traffic queues to the office. Sarah's first thought was that if he spent that much time sitting in queues to the office, how much time did he spend in traffic queues in other places? At that point Sarah knew that she did not want the job.

Sarah knew that one of the 'I really do not want' elements of her There & Then was to be spending hour after hour sat in a car on the M25, or anywhere else for that matter.

For Sarah this was such a key point that it took precedence over all of the positives that she had identified. Of course the opposite could also be true: it could be that there is one positive element of the job that totally overrides any of the downsides.

2 Detailed analysis

Okay, so you have done a quick high-level analysis and you have decided that you still have one or more options that you want to take a closer look at. You now need to do some detailed analysis of those options. We have a particular model that we like to use for this – the *So What? Model*. This model is useful for taking what appear to be large-scale changes and issues and breaking them down into smaller and smaller chunks until all you are left with is a list of easy-to-handle actions, lots of small steps that, when put together, make up a giant leap! Always consider your career ideas in terms of your long-term goals.

Make sure that whatever options you are looking at are related to your There & Then at every stage. If we continue with the Marketing theme, let's say that in going into Marketing we are going to have to learn six new skills. Fine. However, what if only three of them are relevant to the long-term There & Then that we are trying to achieve? That means that we will be expending a lot of time and effort in learning three things that we do not need in the long term. At this stage you might decide that it would be better to try to find some other way of developing the three skills that you do need. Be flexible, be open-minded and *be totally selfish!*

It may be in this case that you do have to go ahead and learn all six skills, that there is no alternative route. So be it. Accept it as the price you have to pay to develop the three skills that you do need.

So, how does the So What? Model work? It's very simple really.

1 Take the career option that you are looking at (we'll continue to use Marketing).

2 Ask yourself the question 'So what?' – what do you need to do to get there? The answer may be that, 'If I go into Marketing, I am going to have to re-train.'

3 Take each of these things you will need to do to get there in turn and ask yourself again 'So what?' So against 'Training' you will need to think about what training is required and what skills you already have that may be appropriate, and what that training will affect in your life (your finances, social life and home life, etc.).

4 Against each of these headings (finances, social life, home life, etc.) ask yourself 'So what?' How will each be affected?

5 And so on, until all that you are left with is a list of simple things to do – an easy-to-follow Action Plan and a list of any obstacles and implications that will have to be overcome.

6 Once you have this, you can start taking one or more actions to complete every day. As you tick them off your list, you will find that more and more of the larger-scale questions are being answered. For example, by completing all the actions in the 'Training' section you will be able to start acting and updating your skill set – moving towards your goal.

We think it best that we show you what we mean. What we have here are three examples of the So What? Model in tabular form. The first example is about Marketing, the second about being an Independent Consultant and the third about joining the Army as an officer. Please note that these examples are not exhaustive, there will be gaps, but they are here for demonstration purposes. When you come to using the table you will have to be very much more thorough.

Note the difference between the left-hand column and the right-hand column: the former is a big step, a big change that will be both scary and intimidating; the latter is just a series of simple tasks, each of which can be completed quickly and easily, most of them taking no more than a few minutes.

SO WHAT? 1 Marketing

Career Idea	So What?	So What?	So What?	So What?	Actions
Marketing	Training	What training is required? What do I already have?	◆ Can I get training in-house (i.e. does my company have a marketing education programme)? What external options are there? ◆ Need to ask Chartered Institute of Marketing (CIM). Are there any other options: secondments, work experience, etc.? ◆ Is there any literature or are there any journals/magazines that I should read?	◆ Duration (how long to complete)? Compare full- and part-time study, day release and on-the-job training and any other alternatives. ◆ Cost (do I have to pay?) ◆ CIM contact phone number? ◆ If external – can I get funding from work? Where is the best place to study? ◆ Who is the best contact in our Marketing Department? ◆ Do I have anyone in my 'Network' who can help or advise me?	◆ Phone Chartered Institute of Marketing for information. ◆ Speak to Marketing team leader for advice and to look at opportunities. ◆ Check details of internal programmes. ◆ Rewrite CV/application form. ◆ Speak to own team leader about working on projects with Marketing bias. ◆ Check my Network. ◆ Read appropriate literature (library or Marketing team).
	Career Development	◆ Where does this take me? Does it fit my long-term plan? ◆ May mean a backward step.	◆ Need to confirm that all skills are relevant to long-term plan – may only need some elements. ◆ May mean starting again from the bottom. ◆ Need to consider fit of existing skills and experience.	◆ Review long-term plan and compare skills required with new skills learnt if trained in Marketing. ◆ Consider personal implications of loss of responsibility and perhaps position. ◆ Review existing skills and CV.	◆ Get a list of what new skills will be learnt – from Marketing team or Chartered Institute of Marketing. ◆ Update/review list of existing skills. ◆ Review list of skills needed to meet long-term plan.

↑

SO WHAT? 1 Marketing (*continued*)

Career Idea	So What?	So What?	So What?	So What?	Actions
Financial	◆ Starting at the bottom may mean a cut in salary.	◆ Consider minimum earning level required (family, mortgage, loans, etc.). ◆ Speak to CIM and Marketing team about expected earning levels.	◆ Do opportunities exist which will allow me to meet my minimum earning level?		◆ Review minimum earning level. ◆ Speak to Chartered Institute of Marketing and Marketing team about expected earning levels as new Marketer.
Social/ Home	◆ Follows on from Financial and Training.	◆ If taking a drop in salary, what is the effect on social/ home life? ◆ If studying in own time, or taking time out to study full-time, what are the implications for social/home life?			◆ Assess financial status and desired standard of living. ◆ Assess time constraints.
Other	◆ Anything else considered appropriate or specific to the job.	◆ Example: new career, if undertaken, may mean being away from home a lot.			

SO WHAT? 2 Independent Consultant

Career Idea	So What?	So What?	So What?	So What?	Actions
Independent Consultant	Training	What training is required? What do I already have? What skills and experience will clients look for? What skills will I need to operate independently? What will be my specialism?	• Can I get the training, skills and experience I need in my current role? • Are there any other options: secondments, work experience, etc.? • Is there any literature or are there any journals/magazines that I should read? • Whom can I approach for advice about this? (Network and Institute of Management Consultants [IMC].) • Do I know any Independent Consultants who can advise me on how to get started?	• Duration (how long to complete)? Compare full- and part-time study, day release and evening classes, on-the-job training and any other alternatives. • Cost (do I have to pay?)? • IMC contact phone number? • If external – can I get funding from work? Where is the best place to study? • Who is the best consultant contact that I have? • Do I have anyone in my 'Network' who can help or advise me?	• Phone IMC for information. • Speak to Consultants for advice and to look at opportunities. • Check details of internal opportunities and programmes. • Rewrite CV/application form. • Speak to own team leader about working on projects with Consultancy bias. • Check my Network. • Read appropriate literature (library or consulting team).
	Career Development	Where does this take me? Does it fit my long-term plan? May mean a backward step. What effect would an	• Need to confirm that all skills are relevant to long-term plan – may only need some elements. • May mean starting again from the bottom. • Need to consider fit of existing skills and experience. • Is there a market for my	• Review long-term plan and compare skills required with new skills learnt if working independently. • Consider personal implications of loss of stability, responsibility and, perhaps, position.	• Get a breakdown of skills needed to act (1) as a Consultant and (2) independently. • Update/review list of existing skills. • Review list of skills needed to meet long-term plan.

Career Idea	So What?	So What?	So What?	So What?	Actions
	economic slump or recession have?	specialism? What brand do I need to use? Environmental scan needed.	Review existing skills and CV. Need to do some market research. Need to do some competitor analysis.		◆ Approach market research agents, or do it myself by visiting libraries, using internet, etc. ◆ Study competitor websites, literature, etc. ◆ Attend trade conferences, etc, to learn more about market, competitors and customers.
Financial	◆ Starting at the bottom may mean a cut in salary. ◆ Start-up costs for independent.	◆ Consider minimum earning level required (family, mortgage, loans, etc). ◆ Speak to other independents about costs involved. ◆ Ask Financial Advisor about small business opportunities/investors.	◆ Do opportunities exist which will allow me to meet my minimum earning level?		◆ Review minimum earning level. ◆ Speak to other independents about expected earning levels at start-up.
Social/ Home	◆ Follows on from Financial and Training.	◆ If taking a drop in salary what is the effect on social/home life? ◆ If studying in own time, or taking time out to study full time, what are the implications for social/home life?			◆ Assess financial status and desired standard of living. ◆ Assess time constraints.
Other	◆ Anything else considered appropriate or specific to the job.	◆ Example: new career, if undertaken, may mean being away from home a lot.			

SO WHAT? 3 Army Officer

Career Idea	So What?	So What?	So What?	So What?	Actions
Army Officer	Training	What training is required? What do I already have?	Where is the training done? How long does it last for? What is involved? Is there a difference between reservists (TA) and regular officer training? Where can I find more information?	Where can I find out about the selection process? How do I apply? Where can I find out about officer training? What is my commitment to the service once my training is complete? Who do I know in the TA or the regular army? What can I read or do to improve my level of understanding?	Contact my local recruitment office. Contact Royal Military Academy Sandhurst (RMAS) to find out about open days. Visit local TA centre. Visit local regiments. Start fitness programme. Read appropriate books and literature.
	Career Development	Where does this take me? Does it fit my long-term plan? May mean a backward step.	What commitment do I have once my training is complete? (How long do I have to stay for?) What transferable skills will being an Army Officer give me? What effect will military service have on my Network?	Review long-term plan and compare the skills required with the skills learnt during military service. Who do I already know who has military experience? What is the commitment for a TA officer?	Get a list of the skills and experiences gained from being an Army Officer. Speak to recruitment office, local regiment or RMAS about career planning. Confirm length of commitment for regular and TA officers.

SO WHAT? 3 Army Officer (continued)

Career Idea	So What?	So What?	So What?	So What?	Actions
Financial	Starting at the bottom may mean a cut in salary.	Consider minimum earning level required (family, mortgage, loans, etc.).	Do opportunities exist which will allow you to meet your minimum earning level? What is earning level whilst at RMAS? What is earning level on commissioning? What outgoings will I have during training and on commissioning? What is earning level in TA?		Review minimum earning level. Get salary and expenditure forecasts from advisors.
Social/ Home	Follows on from Financial and Training.	If taking a drop in salary, what is the effect on social/home life? Implications of being away from home for extended periods of time? With TA, implications of weekends being given over to training?	What am I prepared to give up, both socially and at home, to pursue a military career?		Assess financial status and desired standard of living. Assess constraints of being away from home for long periods.
Other	Anything else you consider appropriate or specific to the job.	Example: new career, if undertaken, may mean being away from home a lot. In this case may also mean putting oneself at risk.			

The So What? Model is our suggested way of doing things. We have been using it for over four years and the consensus of opinion is that *it works!* The important thing is that you need to do this detailed research and planning to understand what is required and what the price is that you may have to pay.

EXERCISE

If you have come up with a job or role that you think will help you to achieve your There & Then, get some paper and start breaking it down using the So What? Model.

Does it raise questions you had not thought of before? Does it help you set goals and targets (small steps) towards achieving your ultimate aim?

Reality check

For all this to work you have to take ownership and responsibility for what you're doing. Clichéd as it may be, the more effort you put in and the more you take ownership, the more it becomes *your* career plan, for *you*!

It takes time and effort. The more time and effort you give at this planning stage, the more you will reap the benefits in the long run.

If you take nothing else from this book, take the So What? Model. It works for career planning, project assessments, corporate planning and house moving. In fact, it works for everything that involves change.

What's the price?

What are you giving up?

We've mentioned before the effects that change can have on you and those around you. You need to consider how to make a change in such a way as to make it last, make it sustainable. Change happens on various levels ranging from hard and tangible (e.g. buying a new computer) to soft and intangible (e.g. changing the culture of a business). We need to be aware of the level of change that we are trying to introduce for You plc and what the implications are of changing at that level. This can best be introduced using the Change Ladder from Carmel McConnell and Mick Cope's *Float You*, which we've summarized briefly below.

The change ladder

The 'change ladder' has five 'rungs' or levels of change spanning from tangible at the base to intangible at the top (see Figure 7.1). As a tool, the change ladder enables you to focus on the particular levels at which you are trying to make a change while also allowing you to consider the implications at the other levels of the ladder. You should think about each of your big changes in this way.

The advantage of the change ladder is that, once you have mapped what you wish to do, all the different variables can be seen. This can enable you to focus on one change element at a time, or ascertain the linkages between the different elements on the ladder. This ensures that a more holistic view is taken of the change. This is important because, invariably, a change on any one rung of the ladder *will* result in an impact on one or more of the other rungs.

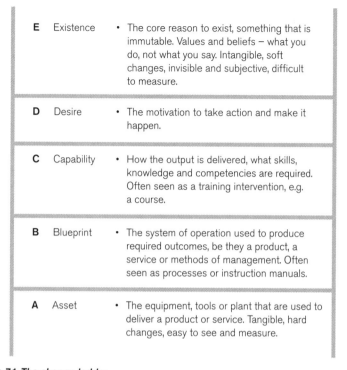

E	Existence	• The core reason to exist, something that is immutable. Values and beliefs – what you do, not what you say. Intangible, soft changes, invisible and subjective, difficult to measure.
D	Desire	• The motivation to take action and make it happen.
C	Capability	• How the output is delivered, what skills, knowledge and competencies are required. Often seen as a training intervention, e.g. a course.
B	Blueprint	• The system of operation used to produce required outcomes, be they a product, a service or methods of management. Often seen as processes or instruction manuals.
A	Asset	• The equipment, tools or plant that are used to deliver a product or service. Tangible, hard changes, easy to see and measure.

Figure 7.1 *The change ladder*

Let us give you a couple of examples:

Example 1: Asset-level change
Let's say that we decide to buy a new computer for home. Easy, an asset intervention: go and buy it and start using it. But it's not that simple. The impact of this change on the other rungs can be seen below:

B Blueprint level. You need instructions to enable you to set the computer up. You need to know the processes for accessing the software installed on the computer.

C Capability level. You may need some training on how to use the software packages on the computer.

D Desire level. You've actually got to want to use the computer once it's set up, otherwise what's the point of having it?

E Existence level. Have you bought the computer because you feel you should have one, or is it because you recognize that it will add value to your lifestyle and will be something that you will use regularly?

Example 2: Existence-level change

For this one, we have just completed the There & Then tools and we realize that we need to make some changes to the Brand we have identified for You plc. This is an E-level intervention, one we have to live every day without question. It has to be second nature to us in everything we do and say. Thus its impact on the other rungs is:

D **Desire level.** You may know that you need to make the change, but do you want to do it? This might mean having to start managing your network more robustly and this could be a character shift that you don't want to undertake.

C **Capability level.** You may need to develop some new skills and capabilities to be able to live your brand.

B **Blueprint level.** You need to understand how you are going to make this change happen, the processes you are going to follow to ensure that it is delivered and maintained.

A **Asset level.** You will need to ensure that you have the kit you require to be able to live the brand – everything from technical equipment (computer, mobile phone, or any specialist kit for your role) to the clothes you wear. Be prepared to change your wardrobe!

To get you started we have mapped on to the ladder *some* of the questions that you might need to answer when making any personal change.

EXERCISE

Think about a change that you are trying to make, or have made recently. Map it against the change ladder.

At what level did you make a change?

What did you do to address the needs at the other levels of the ladder?

E Existence	• What will the impact be on my partner? • What will the impact be on the children? • What will the impact be on immediate family and friends? • Will there be an impact on my health? • Does this violate any of my ethics?
D Desire	• Do I want this badly enough? • Does this fit with my values?
C Capability	• What qualifications will be required? • What additional training is needed? • What skills and experience are required? • Do I have them? Where can I get them?
B Blueprint	• Does the change require some in-depth knowledge or competence? • What environment am I going to make this change in? • Can I manage this and control how I proceed? What planning is required? • Will I need to move location?
A Asset	• What finance will be required? • Will I be lowering my income and therefore my standard of living? • What is the minimum level of income needed? • How much time will I need to invest? • What equipment will I need?

Figure 7.2 *The change ladder questions*

In this chapter we have talked about the need to use what you have learned from Here & Now and There & Then to start identifying the gaps that need to be Bridged. We have also looked at how you can use the results to consider options for development in the future and to help you on your way to the career and lifestyle that you want.

But before you do anything you *must* ensure that you:

◆ Plan your way forward thoroughly. The more you know and the more robust your planning, the better the outcome will be.

- Do some robust analysis, starting at the high level as a simple, early sifting process, before using the So What? Model for a more detailed look at the more serious options you have identified.

- Understand the change that you are making and its implications. You need to know what the price is that you will have to pay.

Through all of this, remember that it is a fast-moving world, so be flexible, be prepared to alter direction and be prepared to face up to all aspects of change. It's better to understand what the price is and make the decision to pay it willingly, rather than not seeing it coming and paying it unwillingly.

Now it is up to you to map what you need to do and assess the price you are willing to pay.

chapter eight
the end or the beginning?

Is this the end?

Yes and no. Yes, it is the end of the book (almost), and it is also the end of getting you to the Here & Now that you have today. No, in that this is not the end of the process.

Recap

We are going to assume that you have worked through the tools and that, hopefully, as a result we will have achieved a number of things together. Here's what you should have by now:

◆ You will have a better understanding of who you are, what is important to you, your skills, your values and how others see you: your Here & Now.

◆ You will have defined a vision for your future, the elements that constitute it, the steps you need to take to get there and when you will achieve it by: your There & Then.

◆ You will have started to look at the gaps between Here & Now and There & Then and, by using the So What? Model, will have started to plan and build the Bridge between the two.

◆ You will know You plc better than anyone else in the world. You will know what your brand is and will be starting to live it.

◆ You will be more aware of the environment in which you operate on a daily basis and will keep updating that awareness.

We must admit that we haven't been able to cover specific situations, so we have concentrated on giving you generic tools that should enable you to start analyzing yourself and planning a better future. We hope that you will have found what we have given you both useful and thought-provoking. If you have taken just one thing from this book, it's been worth it.

It seems so simple, but will it work? A warning

We cannot make you put in the thorough analyses needed here, we cannot make you keep on top of your game and we cannot make you believe in yourself. Only you can do these things and make your change a success. If you believe that you can achieve the There & Then that you have defined, then our belief is that you can get there.

Unless *you* believe in what you are doing and believe that you are capable of achieving it, you are likely to fail. No-one knows you better than you know yourself. Only you will know whether the There & Then you have defined is truly achievable. If you have been honest with yourself and thorough with the exercises and tools you've completed, you have nothing to fear.

Reality, as you probably know, rarely meets our expectations. There is always something that can be changed for the better, particularly in a world that moves as fast as this one does. That is why this career planning process is *not* something that can be completed once and left alone. It is a snapshot in time, and in these fast times things change – you change! You need to get into the habit of taking the picture at regular intervals, updating your Here & Now in response to changes in your values, changed environmental issues and changes in your life. Then you need to reflect on There & Then and your plan for getting there, and change it as necessary.

Be flexible!
Be prepared to change your plan!
Be totally selfish!

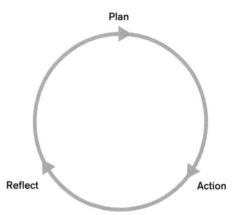

Figure 8.1 *The action circle*

You need to Plan, Action, Reflect and Plan again (Figure 8.1). What we have shown you is that you need to be constantly planning (using the tools), taking action to bridge the gap, then reflecting on what has happened before building that into the next round of planning. Do this effectively and you can alter your plans to produce better outcomes, or outcomes more applicable to your situation and environment at that time. The path is not always smooth, but you can be better prepared for the bumps along the way if you have put the effort in beforehand.

What use is all this? Some ideas

Hopefully, as you have worked your way through the book, you will have appreciated that these tools can be used to help you in a number of ways. Here are some of them:

In the corporate world to:

- develop personal development plans;
- conduct personal development reviews;
- plan your training for the coming year;
- assess your current performance;
- decide what you want from life.

In the free agent world to:

- develop your brand and brand values;
- position your brand and market yourself effectively;
- define from your values, your unique proposition;
- determine the skills you are able to bring to market;
- understand where you are and what you require from life;
- understand the impact of the environment.

Of course, taken on their own, the ideas contained within this book do exactly what it says on the cover: they enable you to Be Your Own Career Consultant. Will they work? *Yes!* What use are they? Used properly, they can enable you to take ownership and control of your career planning, your future, and link it with your lifestyle requirements and the environment in which you are operating and living.

A final reality check

Any tool is only as good as the worker who is using it. This book and the ideas and tools contained within it are for you to work with as you try to be the best that you can be. If you want to realize your potential, you must use the tools you have properly to get the best out of them. *Do not cut corners. It's your future and it's too important!*

Be thorough, be robust – if necessary, be brutally honest with yourself and encourage others to do the same. You will then find that the There & Then that you define is SMART and IDEAL. Don't cheat yourself. Go and do something you only ever dreamed of!

There is something else that you should look out for: people normally think about career planning when they are upset, are frustrated and hate their job, their boss, the company and the whole world! Don't fall into this trap! Make time for career planning, especially when things are going really well. That is the time that you will come up with the more inspirational ideas, the ones that will take You plc on to a brighter future. The constant management of your career is what creates results.

Remember that all the reflection and all the planning in the world lead to nothing unless you are prepared to take some action.

If you keep on doing what you have always done you will get what you have always got.

We also hope that we have given you something to work on here. If we have, if you're struggling with any part of the book, or if you have a story that you want to share with us, then you can send us your thoughts at the momentum website (***www.yourmomentum.com***) through the contacts section in the menu. We would very much like to hear from you.

'If you can dream it, you can do it.'

Walt Disney

As we reach the end of the book, remember that this is not the end, just the end of the beginning. If you have defined your Here & Now, we guarantee that it will be out of date very, very soon, if it isn't already. In these fast times you have to keep on top of it, review it constantly and update it as necessary. If you have completed everything in the book, then go and pick one of the tools at random and do it again. See if it has changed. Then try another. If you are still not sure, go back and start again – it's amazing what a good night's sleep will do. If you are sure and now know what you want to do, *go do it*.

We want you to have a different life: one that motivates you, one that inspires you and lifts you above the norm. We want you to be bursting at the seams every day with ideas and dreams. We want you to be passionate about You plc, to recognize that you own it, that you're responsible for it and that you can enable it to develop in any way you wish.

Let's make You plc the place that everyone else wants to work, and let's do it now!

sites of interest

Since we have given you a lot to think about, as it all settles down you may be interested in looking at the following:

◆ www.authorminds.com

◆ www.business-minds.com

◆ www.fastcompany.com (unit of one and free agent)

◆ www.financialminds.com

◆ www.global-insight.com (personal knowledge management)

◆ www.tompeters.com (branding)

◆ www.traininguniversity.com (training ideas and information)

◆ www.wizoz.co.uk (change, change ladder and personal capital)

◆ www.yourmomentum.com

There are also numerous other employment sites that offer career advice. These cover testing, CVs, adverts and some aspects of self-assessment.

further reading

Given the fact that we have given you a lot to think about, as it all settles down you may be interested in looking at the following:

◆ Bach, Richard, *Jonathan Livingston Seagull*, HarperCollins, 1994

◆ Bolles, Richard Nelson, *What Color Is Your Parachute?*, Ten Speed Press, 1998

◆ Cope, Mick, *The Seven Cs of Consulting*, Pearson Education Limited, 2000

◆ Covey, Stephen R., *7 Habits of Highly Effective People*, Simon & Schuster, 1989

◆ *Fast Company Magazine*, Gruner & Jahr USA Publishing, Monthly

◆ Geus, Arie de, *The Living Company*

◆ Grant, Tony and Greene, Jane, *Coach Yourself: Make Real Change in Your Life*, momentum, 2001

◆ McConnell, Carmel and Cope, Mick, *Float You: How to Capitalize on Your Talent*, momentum, 2001

◆ Morito, Akio, *Made in Japan*, HarperCollins, 1987

◆ Peters, Tom, *The Brand You 50*, Alfred A. Knopf, 1999

◆ Pink, Daniel H., *Free Agent Nation: How America's New Independent Workers Are Transforming the Way We Live*, Warner Books, 2001

◆ Quinn, Barbara, *Snap, Crackle or Stop: Change Your Career and Create Your Own Destiny*, momentum, 2001

- Ridderstrale, Jonas and Nordstrom, Kjell, *Funky Business*, ft.com, 2000

- Schien, Edgar H., *Career Anchors: Discovering Your Real Values*, Jossey-Bass, Pfeiffer & Co., 1990

- Wright, Bridget, *Career Shift*, Piatkus, 1993

f u r t h e r   r e a d i n g

momentum prescription – Let Us Help You Work Out Which Book Will Suit Your Symptoms

Feel stuck in a rut? Something wrong and need help doing something about it?

◆ If you need tools to help making changes in your life: **coach yourself** (a good general guide to change)

◆ If you are considering dramatic career change: **snap, crackle or stop**

◆ If you need to work out what you'd like to be doing and how to get there: **be your own career consultant**

◆ If you need help making things happen and tackling the 'system' at work/in life: **change activist**

Feel that you can never make decisions and you just let things 'happen'?

◆ If you need help making choices: **the big difference**

◆ If you want to feel empowered and start making things happen for yourself: **change activist**

Feel life is too complicated and overwhelming?

◆ If you need help working through office politics and complexity: **clued up**

◆ If you need a kick up the backside to get out of your commerce-induced coma: **change activist**

◆ If you need an amusing and very helpful modern life survival guide: **innervation**

◆ If you never have enough time or energy to get things done or think properly: **mental space**

Feel like you might be in the wrong job?

◆ If you want help finding your destiny job and inspiration to make that dramatic career change: **snap, crackle or stop**

◆ If you feel like you aren't doing a job that is really 'what you are about': **soultrader**

◆ If you are struggling with the 'do something worthwhile OR make money dilemma': **change activist**

Feel that you're not the person/leader you should be?

◆ If you want to be the kind of person others want to follow: **lead yourself**

◆ If you need help becoming the person you've always wanted to be: **reinvent yourself**

◆ If you want to work out everything you've got to offer, and how to improve that: **grow your personal capital**

Feel you need help getting your ideas into action?

◆ If the problem is mainly other people, lack of time and the messiness of life: **clued up**

◆ If the problem is communicating your thinking: **hey you!**

◆ If the problem is more ideas than time and you are a bit overwhelmed with work: **mental space**

◆ If the problem is making change in your life: **coach yourself**

Feel you aren't projecting yourself and managing your career as well as you should?

◆ If you'd like to be the kind of person people think of first: **managing brand me**

◆ If you'd like people to listen to your ideas more readily: **hey you!**

◆ If you'd like to come across as the person you really are inside: **soultrader**

◆ If you need general help in changing the way you work/life: **coach yourself**

◆ If you need help working out what you've got and how best to use it: **float you**

Feel you'd like to be much more creative and a real 'ideas person'

◆ If you need inspiration on how to be innovative and think creatively: **innervation**

◆ If you need help spreading your ideas and engendering support! **hey you!**